LIVING THROUGH THE VIETNAM WAR

Other books in this series:

LIVING THROUGH THE COLD WAR

LIVING THROUGH THE VIETNAM WAR

Edited by Samuel Brenner

Bruce Glassman, *Vice President*
Bonnie Szumski, *Publisher*
Helen Cothran, *Managing Editor*
Scott Barbour, *Series Editor*

GREENHAVEN PRESS
An imprint of Thomson Gale, a part of The Thomson Corporation

THOMSON

™

GALE

Detroit • New York • San Francisco • San Diego • New Haven, Conn.
Waterville, Maine • London • Munich

THOMSON

★ ™

GALE

© 2005 Thomson Gale, a part of The Thomson Corporation.

Thomson and Star Logo are trademarks and Gale and Greenhaven Press are registered trademarks used herein under license.

For more information, contact
Greenhaven Press
27500 Drake Rd.
Farmington Hills, MI 48331-3535
Or you can visit our Internet site at http://www.gale.com

Cover credit: © Bettmann/CORBIS. A U.S. Marine guards women, children, and elders while their South Vietnamese village is being searched in September 1965.

LIBRARY OF CONGRESS CATALOGING-IN-PUBLICATION DATA

Living through the Vietnam War / Samuel Brenner, book editor.
    p. cm. — (Living through the Cold War)
  Includes bibliographical references and index.
  ISBN 0-7377-2308-4 (lib. : alk. paper)
    1. Vietnamese Conflict, 1961–1975—United States. 2. United States—History—1961–1969. 3. United States—History—1969– . I. Brenner, Samuel. II. Series.

DS558.V558 2005
959.704'3373—dc22   2003062477

Printed in the United States of America

CONTENTS

Chapter 1: Government Statements on Vietnam

Chapter 2: Protesting American Involvement in Vietnam

Chapter 3: Soldiers and Veterans

Americans to leave Saigon as it was captured by the North Vietnamese Army in 1975, he observed the U.S. abandonment of South Vietnam.

A former career U.S. Marine officer explains that he believed that the war was useful and necessary and that the United States entered the conflict with the best of intentions.

Vietnam veteran David Donovan describes the opening of the Vietnam Memorial in Washington, D.C., in 1982, which signaled a new era in America's acknowledgement of the war, and brought a long-awaited sense of closure to many veterans.

Chapter 4: Vietnam in Media and Popular Culture

The former anchor of CBS Evening News who in 1968 had shocked the nation by delivering a short, sharp indictment of the war, describes how he came to be disillusioned with the conflict and how his comments mobilized antiwar feeling.

An antiwar playwright recalls Berkeley and San Francisco at the height of the counterculture in the 1960s and describes her own experiences putting on political, antiwar shows with the San Francisco Mime Troupe.

Individuals react to a televised performance of the antiwar song "I-Feel-Like-I'm-Fixin'-to-Die-Rag," describing it as insensitive and anti-American.

At the midpoint of the Cold War, in early 1968, U.S. television viewers saw surprising reports from Vietnam, where American ground troops had been fighting since 1965. They learned that South Vietnamese Communist rebels, known as the Vietcong, had attacked unexpectedly throughout the country. At one point Vietcong insurgents engaged U.S. troops and officials in a firefight at the very center of U.S. power in Vietnam, the American embassy in South Vietnam's capital, Saigon. Meanwhile, thousands of soldiers and marines faced a concerted siege at Khe Sanh, an isolated base high in central Vietnam's mountains. Their adversary was not the Vietcong, but rather the regular North Vietnamese army.

Reporters and U.S. citizens quickly learned that these events constituted the Tet Offensive, a coordinated attack by Vietnamese Communists that occurred in late January, the period of Tet, Vietnam's new year. The American public was surprised by the Tet Offensive because they had been led to believe that the United States and its South Vietnamese allies were winning the war, that Vietcong forces were weak and dwindling, and that the massive buildup of American forces (there were some five hundred thousand U.S. troops in Vietnam by early 1968), ensured that the south would remain free of a Communist takeover. Since 1965, politicians, pundits, and generals had claimed that massive American intervention was justified and that the war was being won. On a publicity tour in November 1967 General William Westmoreland, the American commander in Vietnam, had assured officials and reporters that "the ranks of the Vietcong are thinning steadily" and that "we have reached a point where the end begins to come into view." President Lyndon B. Johnson's advisers, meanwhile, continually encouraged him to publicly emphasize "the light at the end of the tunnel."

Ordinary Americans had largely supported the troop build-up in Vietnam, believing the argument that the country was an important front in the Cold War, the global effort to stop the spread of communism that had begun in the late 1940s. Communist regimes already held power in nearby China, North Korea, and in northern Vietnam; it was deemed necessary to hold the line in the south not only to prevent communism from taking hold there but to prevent other nations from falling to communism throughout Asia. In 1965, polls showed that 80 percent of Americans believed that intervention in Vietnam was justified despite the fact that involvement in this fight would alter American life in numerous ways. For example, young men faced the possibility of being drafted and sent to fight—and possibly die—in a war thousands of miles away. As the war progressed, citizens watched more and more of their sons—both draftees and enlisted men—being returned to the United States in coffins (approximately fifty-eight thousand Americans died in Vietnam). Antiwar protests roiled college campuses and sometimes the streets of major cities. The material costs of the war threatened domestic political reforms and America's economic health, offering the continuing specter of rising taxes and shrinking services. Nevertheless, as long as the fight was succeeding, a majority of Americans could accept these risks and sacrifices.

Tet changed many minds, suggesting as it did that the war was not, in fact, going well. When CBS news anchor Walter Cronkite, who was known as "the most trusted man in America," suggested in his broadcast on the evening of February 27 that the Vietnam War might be unwinnable and could only end in a stalemate, many people wondered if he might be right and began to suspect that the positive reports from generals and politicians might have been misleading. It was a turning point in the battle for public opinion. Johnson reportedly said that Cronkite's expressions of doubt signaled the loss of mainstream America's support for the war. Indeed, after Tet more and more people joined Cronkite in wondering whether fighting this obscure enemy in an isolated country halfway around the world was worth the cost—whether it was a truly important front in the Cold War. They made their views known through demonstrations and opinion polls, and politicians were forced to respond. In a dramatic and unexpected turn of events, Johnson declined to run for reelection in 1968, stating that his involvement in the political campaign would detract from his efforts to negotiate a peace agreement with North Vietnam. His successor, Richard Nixon, won the election after promising to end the war.

The Tet Offensive and its consequences provide strong examples of how the Cold War touched the lives of ordinary Americans. Far from being an abstract geopolitical event, the Cold War, as Tet reveals, was an ever-present influence in the everyday life of the nation. Greenhaven Press's Living Through the Cold War series provides snapshots into the lives of ordinary people during the Cold War, as well as their reactions to its major events and developments. Each volume is organized around a particular event or distinct stage of the Cold War. Primary documents such as eyewitness accounts and speeches give firsthand insights into both ordinary peoples' experiences and leaders' decisions. Secondary sources provide factual information and place events within a larger global and historical context. Additional resources include a detailed introduction, a comprehensive chronology, and a thorough bibliography. Also included are an annotated table of contents and a detailed index to help the reader locate information quickly. With these features, the Living Through the Cold War series reveals the human dimension of the superpower rivalry that defined the globe during most of the latter half of the twentieth century.

On the night of August 28, 1968, thousands of protesters ringed the meeting hall of the Democratic National Convention in Chicago chanting, "Death to the pigs" and "Fascist bastards!" As inside the hall delegates cast votes to decide who would be the Democratic Party's presidential candidate in the fall election, Mayor Richard J. Daley's police charged the demonstrators, firing tear gas, clubbing protesters to the ground, and in some cases shouting, "Kill, kill!"[1] The violence broke out as the television networks were prepared to go on air with the scene from the convention floor, where then–vice president Hubert Humphrey was about to be nominated; instead, the networks focused for twenty minutes on the brutality taking place just outside of the building. Millions of Americans were shocked to see how law and order was breaking down in one of America's major cities, literally next to the convention of the most powerful political party in the country. Almost as disturbing as the police violence to many Americans were the images of hippies and foul-mouthed, long-haired antiwar activists burning American flags and verbally trashing the U.S. government. The violence in Chicago was emblematic of the Vietnam era. This event illustrates the breakdown in law and order, the intensity of emotion generated by the war, the clash between the establishment and counterculture—all of which were characteristic of this momentous period. The Vietnam War had many long-term consequences for the nation. Three of the most significant were its impact on U.S. foreign policy, on American self-confidence, and on citizens' perceptions of the political process.

The Lessons of Vietnam

The Vietnam era drastically changed how the United States interacted with other nations throughout the remainder of the

11

twentieth century. As historian George C. Herring argues, "Nowhere was the impact of Vietnam greater than on the nation's foreign policy. The war shattered the consensus that had existed since the late 1940s, leaving Americans confused and deeply divided over the goals to be pursued and the methods used."[2] The United States entered the Vietnam era dedicated to containing communism and what Americans saw as the forces of evil everywhere in the world. By the end of the era, however, after the losses of the war and the horrific social stresses of the period, the country had abandoned its complete dedication to the doctrine of containment along with much of its confidence in American military power as the answer to ideological questions.

The concept of containment can be traced to what policy experts call "the lessons of Munich." Munich was the city in which Great Britain made a pre–World War II attempt to satisfy Adolf Hitler by essentially allowing Germany to invade and conquer Czechoslovakia. The British hoped that by giving Hitler something he wanted, they could appease the homicidal dictator. As the British soon discovered, however, Hitler saw their surrender as a sign that he could demand even more territory and that the Allies would do nothing to stop him. The lessons of Munich, then, were that free countries should not try to appease tyrants and conquerors. American strategists sought to apply the lessons of Munich to the Cold War; they formulated the policy of containment, under which America would not attempt to destroy the Soviet Union but would act to prevent the Soviets from expanding their borders or exporting communism around the world. These strategists reasoned that giving up so much as a single yard of territory would send the message that the Soviet Union could demand and take even more territory with impunity. Thus, they committed America to a course of preventing a Communist takeover of South Vietnam.

The Vietnam-era American strategists sought to apply the lessons of Munich to the Vietnam conflict but found that Southeast Asia was very different from pre–World War II Europe. The U.S. defeat in Vietnam left American leaders with a new set of lessons. The lessons of Vietnam were that the United

States could not continue to act as the world's policeman, as it had since World War II; that American troops should never be committed to battle without clear objectives and a clear exit strategy; and that even American military power could not triumph when it was opposed both by the people in the territories the United States was seeking to "liberate" and by many of the American people at home. These lessons have been applied to all subsequent U.S. military intervention, with U.S. leaders vigilantly avoiding the creation of "another Vietnam."

National Confidence

Bedsides leaving U.S. officials wary of leading the nation into war, Vietnam left ordinary citizens disillusioned about their country. Americans after World War II had been generally optimistic about America's global status and the state of American society. Americans were the triumphant victors of World War II, and in many cases they saw themselves as the protectors of democracy, freedom, and human dignity. Americans were, many believed, citizens of the most powerful, united, prosperous, and advanced nation in the world. American society in the period before the Vietnam era was, of course, not perfect. Many Americans had been angered and scared by the excesses of Senator Joseph McCarthy's Communist-hunting House Un-American Activities Committee, which was active during the 1950s. Claiming that the U.S. government had been infiltrated by Communist agents, McCarthy had tracked down Americans who had been in any way involved with communism at any time and essentially destroyed their lives by publicly humiliating them and making it impossible for them to find employment. At the same time, a great many Americans (especially African Americans) remained poor and discriminated against by the racist Jim Crow laws of the South. Martin Luther King Jr.'s famous civil rights marches had not yet occurred, and in much of the South, African Americans were prevented from voting and were not even permitted to use the same drinking fountains, bathrooms, or bus seats as Caucasians. Running throughout the period was the overwhelming fear in the country that the Soviet Union might succeed in defeating the United States in war or outdistancing the United States in science or culture. The Soviet string of "firsts" in the space race, for instance—including the first satellite to orbit the earth and the first man in space—continued to underline the fact that early American spacecraft routinely exploded on the launch pads. Despite these concerns, Americans had nonetheless retained their confidence in the ultimate power and righteousness of their country.

By the end of the Vietnam era, however, much of the nation's confidence had been left in the streets of Saigon and on the battlefields of Southeast Asia. Regardless of their views on the causes of the defeat in Vietnam, and regardless of whether they supported U.S. involvement in Southeast Asia, many Americans were shocked by America's failure to win the war. How, they wondered, could the United States be the greatest and most powerful country in the world if it lacked either the military power or the political will to defeat a significantly less powerful enemy? How could the United States be the most advanced and united country in the world if its population could abandon American soldiers, riot in cities, attack police officers in the streets, and mock and disobey the government? While many Americans remained proud of their country and opposed to communism, it was clear during the Vietnam period that American optimism had taken a serious blow. As historian James T. Patterson argues, the Vietnam War "called into question the honor and decency of much that Americans claimed to stand for."[3]

Political Engagement and the Credibility Gap

The Vietnam era also witnessed a change in the way many ordinary citizens perceived and interacted with the U.S. government. While not all Americans blindly obeyed the government before the period, many ordinary American citizens entered the era as generally unquestioning supporters of government officials and policies. In essence, these Americans were silent observers of the political process. Although some Americans responded to the political upheavals of the Vietnam period by becoming cynical and by withdrawing entirely from the politi-

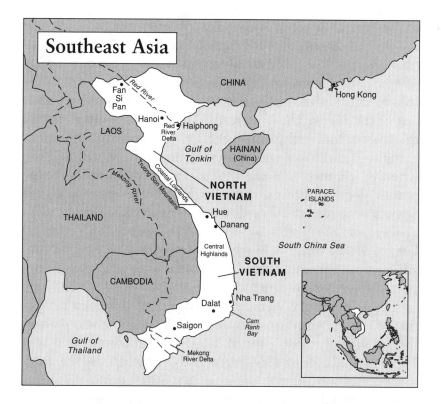

Southeast Asia

cal community, the period tended to encourage political activism. Hundreds of thousands of Americans participated in or opposed the mass protest marches of 1965 through 1968, including the one-hundred-thousand-person October 1967 march on the Pentagon in Washington, D.C. Increased political involvement was particularly noticeable on the nation's college campuses, where organizations such as Students for a Democratic Society and the much larger conservative, largely prowar Young Americans for Freedom mobilized hundreds of thousands of supporters, speakers, and protesters. Many formerly silent or uninterested observers thus emerged from the era as advocates of participatory democracy, eager to have their voices heard and their presence felt in the halls of the nation's capitol and throughout the ranks of government.

One of the most important and striking transformations of American society in the Vietnam era, and one of the driving forces of this increase in political activism, was the emergence of the "credibility gap"—the disparity between the truth and the official statements of U.S. political leaders. At the beginning of major U.S. military involvement in Vietnam (the early 1960s), Americans tended to believe what they were being told by their government. Even after the questionable activities of the House Un-American Activities Committee during the Joseph McCarthy era of the 1950s—and after President Dwight Eisenhower was caught lying to the world in 1960 when he claimed that the United States was not using spy planes to take pictures of the Soviet Union, after which the Soviets produced the shot-down American pilot Francis Gary Powers—many Americans seemed to believe that political leaders would never willingly and knowingly lie to their constituents. In general, Americans trusted their leaders and supported their government.

The events of the Vietnam era changed this popular perception of governmental trustworthiness. The problem was that, although many (probably most) Americans supported the war in Vietnam until at least 1966 and consequently believed the information they were getting from the administrations of presidents Eisenhower, John F. Kennedy, and Lyndon B. Johnson, events as recorded by newspaper reporters in Vietnam began to bear little resemblance to the events officially described by the government. The most powerful blow to Americans' trust in government came with the Tet Offensive of January 1968. After military and political leaders had spent years telling the American public that the enemy was almost completely defeated, the North Vietnamese and Vietcong guerrillas launched a massive attack on U.S. and South Vietnamese forces, killing and wounding thousands of American soldiers and even gaining access to the American embassy in Saigon. While U.S. forces beat back the attacks with severe losses to the North Vietnamese, the offensive revealed that the government's previous claims about the war seemed to be false. Walter Cronkite, until that time America's most prowar journalist, spoke for many Americans when he turned to an assistant after finishing a report on the Tet Offensive and (while accidentally still on the air) asked, "What the hell is going on? I thought we were winning this war."[4]

The growth of the credibility gap proved disastrous for some American political leaders. As historian Allen J. Matusow argues, "There is no doubt that one of the war's casualties was Lyndon Johnson. Vietnam . . . made him one of the most hated chief executives in a hundred years."[5] The problem of the credibility gap in American politics continued to grow after Richard Nixon was elected in 1968, and it was compounded in 1971 when Daniel Ellsberg, a former marine and State Department official who was working for the RAND Corporation, illegally released what became known as the Pentagon Papers. These papers were initially part of a study commissioned by the secretary of defense on U.S. decision making in Indochina. The authors of the study, who had access to classified information, concluded that U.S. leaders had at times acted both foolishly and dishonestly in communicating to the public about the war in Vietnam, that American troops had been militarily engaged in Vietnam long before the American public had been told of any such engagement, and even that President Johnson had perhaps intentionally lied to Congress when he decided to commit troops after two U.S. destroyers were reportedly attacked by North Vietnamese forces in the Gulf of Tonkin in 1964.

American distrust of government peaked during the Watergate scandal, during which President Nixon tried to cover up evidence that he had been aware of a plan for the Republicans to break into the office of the National Democratic Party on July 17, 1972. Watergate proved to be the final straw for an American public already wounded by and distrustful of the government for its lies about Vietnam. After the Vietnam War and the Nixon presidency, never again would Americans trust their government as they had in the post–World War II era.

A Polarized Nation

On its face the Cold War world was one of black and white. To Americans, it seemed that nations were either on "our side" or on "their side"; while some nations were in the process of deciding which side they would be on, there appeared to be no stable middle ground. Many Americans believed that the

United States and the forces of democracy and liberty were locked in a massive struggle over the fate of humankind with the dark forces of international communism. After the Soviets tested the atom bomb in 1950, the consequences for the losers on either side included total personal and national annihilation. The Vietnam War was an integral part of this black-and-white world and of this global conflict; the transformations the war wrought in national policy and confidence were extreme and lasting. The intense nature of the conflict was reflected in the strong views of those in the United States who supported American involvement in Vietnam and those who opposed it. As historian James T. Patterson explains, "Above all, the war polarized American society."[6]

Americans had entered the Vietnam era on a national "high": America had a booming economy, a trustworthy government, and products and culture that many people considered the best in the world. By the end of the Vietnam period, however, the economy was in desperate shape, many Americans were either shamed or angered by the U.S. failure to win the war in Southeast Asia, the U.S. government was demonstrably lying to American citizens and the world, and American strategists had rejected the lessons of Munich, which were the guiding rules of post–World War II American strategy, in favor of the more cautious lessons of Vietnam.

Notes

1. Lewis L. Gould, *1968: The Election That Changed America*. Chicago: Ivan R. Dee, 1993, p. 130.

2. George C. Herring, *America's Longest War: The United States and Vietnam, 1950–1975*. 3rd ed. New York: McGraw-Hill, 1996, p. 307.

3. James T. Patterson, *Grand Expectations: The United States, 1945–1974*. New York: Oxford University Press, 1996, p. 600.

4. Walter Cronkite, inadvertent broadcast remark, February 1, 1968.

5. Allen J. Matusow, *The Unraveling of America: A History of Liberalism in the 1960s*. New York: Harper & Row, 1984, p. 155.

6. Patterson, *Grand Expectations*, p. 598.

CHAPTER 1

Government Statements on Vietnam

The Justification for War

Lyndon Baines Johnson

The period of greatest U.S. military and political involvement in Southeast Asia—from 1965 through 1972—was in great part sparked by the Gulf of Tonkin incident of August 1964. On August 2, 1964, the U.S. destroyer *Maddox*, which was on a reconnaissance mission in the Gulf of Tonkin, was attacked by three North Vietnamese gunboats, which drove the vessel away from the North Vietnamese island of Hon Me. Although torpedoes were fired at the *Maddox* the ship and crew escaped serious injury. Two days later (August 4), the *Maddox* rejoined another destroyer, the USS *Turner Joy*, in the middle of the Gulf of Tonkin. That evening, from within the middle of a raging storm, the *Turner Joy* reported that it had been fired upon with torpedoes, that it had picked up high-speed vessels on its radar, and that the two vessels were attacking the supposed aggressors. While the *Maddox* participated in the attack, it did not see any such vessels on its radar, and it is possible that the *Turner Joy*'s radar operator was simply seeing radar "ghosts" caused by the storm.

At the time of the reported attacks, the *Maddox* and the *Turner Joy* were in the Gulf of Tonkin, which meant that the destroyers were in international waters (waters that do not belong to any one nation). As the *Maddox* and *Turner Joy* were not invading North Vietnamese waters, it appeared as though North Vietnamese gunboats had without provocation attacked U.S. warships. Such an inten-

Lyndon Baines Johnson, address to the U.S. Congress, Washington, DC, August 5, 1964.

tional, unprovoked attack on the military forces of another nation constitutes an act of war. President Lyndon Baines Johnson had arguably been looking for an excuse to expand the war in Vietnam, and on August 5, he went to the U.S. Congress with a request for a resolution expressing support for "all necessary action to protect our armed forces and to assist [our allies]." In this address, President Johnson explained what he saw as his justifications for war and his plans for the conflict in Southeast Asia. He claimed that the United States had made a commitment to protect South Vietnam from Communist aggression and that a failure to protect that nation could put the freedom of the entire region at risk.

In response to Johnson's request, Congress passed a joint resolution on August 7 (the Gulf of Tonkin Resolution), in which it effectively handed over much of its power to the executive branch of government. The Gulf of Tonkin Resolution made it possible for President Johnson to expand the conflict greatly—in effect to wage war—without returning to Congress for permission. As the key passage of the resolution explained, "That the Congress approves and supports the determination of the President, as Commander in Chief, to take all necessary measures to repel any armed attack against the forces of the United States and to prevent further aggression." The crucial phrase—"all necessary measures"—was left open to presidential interpretation.

L ast night [August 4, 1964] I announced to the American people that the North Vietnamese regime had conducted further deliberate attacks against U.S. naval vessels operating in international waters, and therefore directed air action against gunboats and supporting facilities used in these hostile operations. This air action has now been carried out with substantial damage to the boats and facilities. Two U.S. aircraft were lost in the action.

After consultation with the leaders of both parties in the Congress, I further announced a decision to ask the Congress for a resolution expressing the unity and determination of the

United States in supporting freedom and in protecting peace in southeast Asia.

These latest actions of the North Vietnamese regime have given a new and grave turn to the already serious situation in southeast Asia. Our commitments in that area are well known to the Congress. They were first made in 1954 by President Eisenhower. They were further defined in the Southeast Asia Collective Defense Treaty approved by the Senate in February 1955.

This treaty with its accompanying protocol obligates the United States and other members to act in accordance with their constitutional processes to meet Communist aggression against any of the parties or protocol states.

U.S. Policy in Southeast Asia

Our policy in southeast Asia has been consistent and unchanged since 1954. I summarized it on June 2 in four simple propositions:

1. America keeps her word. Here as elsewhere, we must and shall honor our commitments.

2. The issue is the future of southeast Asia as a whole. A threat to any nation in that region is a threat to all, and a threat to us.

3. Our purpose is peace. We have no military, political, or territorial ambitions in the area.

4. This is not just a jungle war, but a struggle for freedom on every front of human activity. Our military and economic assistance to South Vietnam and Laos in particular has the purpose of helping these countries to repel aggression and strengthen their independence.

The threat to the three nations of southeast Asia has long been clear. The North Vietnamese regime has constantly sought to take over South Vietnam and Laos. This Communist regime has violated the Geneva accords for Vietnam. It has systematically conducted a campaign of subversion, which includes the direction, training, and supply of personnel and arms for the conduct of guerrilla warfare in South Vietnamese territory. In Laos, the North Vietnamese regime has maintained military forces, used Laotian territory for infiltration into South Vietnam, and most recently carried out combat operations—all in direct violation of the Geneva agreements of 1962.

The United States Seeks No Wider War

In recent months, the actions of the North Vietnamese regime have become steadily more threatening. In May, following new acts of Communist aggression in Laos, the United States undertook reconnaissance flights over Laotian territory, at the request of the Government of Laos. These flights had the essential mission of determining the situation in territory where Communist forces were preventing inspection by the International Control Commission. When the Communists attacked these aircraft, I responded by furnishing escort fighters with instructions to fire when fired upon. Thus, these latest North Vietnamese attacks on our naval vessels are not the first direct attack on armed forces of the United States.

As President of the United States I have concluded that I should now ask the Congress on its part, to join in affirming the national determination that all such attacks will be met, and that the United States will continue in its basic policy of assisting the free nations of the area to defend their freedom.

As I have repeatedly made clear, the United States intends no rash-ness, and seeks no wider war. We must make it clear to all that the United States is united in its determination to bring about the end of Communist subversion and aggression in the area. We seek the full and effective restoration of the international agreements signed in Geneva in 1954, with respect to South Vietnam, and again in Geneva in 1962, with respect to Laos.

A Resolution for All Necessary Action

I recommend a resolution expressing the support of the Congress for all necessary action to protect our Armed Forces and to assist nations covered by the SEATO [Southeast Asian Treaty Organization] Treaty. At the same time, I assure the Congress that we shall continue readily to explore any avenues of political solution that will effectively guarantee the removal of Communist subversion and the preservation of the independence of the nations of the area.

The resolution could well be based upon similar resolutions enacted by the Congress in the past—to meet the threat to Formosa [Taiwan] in 1955, to meet the threat to the Middle East in 1957, and to meet the threat in Cuba in 1962. It could state in the simplest terms the resolve and support of the Congress for action to deal appropriately with attacks against our Armed Forces and to defend freedom and preserve peace in southeast Asia in accordance with the obligations of the United States under the Southeast Asia Treaty. I urge the Congress to enact such a resolution promptly and thus to give convincing evidence to the aggressive Communist nations, and to the word as a whole, that our policy in southeast Asia will be carried forward—and that the peace and security of the area will be preserved.

The events of this week would in any event have made the passage of a congressional resolution essential. But there is an additional reason for doing so at a time when we are entering on three months of political campaigning. Hostile nations must understand that in such a period the United States will continue to protect its national interests, and that in these matters there is no division among us.

Seeking Peace in Vietnam

Lyndon Baines Johnson

By the spring of 1968 President Lyndon Baines Johnson was, in many ways, a shattered man. The brilliant and abrasive Texas politician, who had risen through the ranks of the U.S. Senate, had been selected by John Fitzgerald Kennedy as a running mate solely to win the support of the south and had largely been ignored during Kennedy's years in office. Johnson rallied in a masterly fashion after Kennedy's assassination and went on to lead the United States through one of the most remarkable eras of domestic legislation (including civil rights and antipoverty legislation) in American history. His plan for the United States, Johnson had declared soon after Kennedy's death, would lead to a "Great Society" in America. Johnson's attitude and resolve had secured him a massive victory over Arizona senator Barry Goldwater in the presidential election of 1964.

By 1968, however, much of the Great Society legislation had backfired and the nation had been pushed into a period of escalating economic recession—not least because of the astronomical costs of the war in Vietnam. In addition, by 1968 the war had backfired on Johnson's administration. While in 1965 Johnson had promised victory in a year, and then two, and then certainly by 1968, in January 1968 the North Vietnamese and the Vietcong in South Vietnam launched a massive offensive on the Buddhist Tet holiday. This Tet Offensive proved disastrous for the North Vietnamese and Vietcong in purely tactical terms—the Vietcong

Lyndon Baines Johnson, address to the nation, Washington, DC, March 31, 1968.

were essentially wiped out—but shocked the American public, which had believed that the war was essentially over. As more and more Americans came to doubt the Johnson administration's word on Vietnam, Johnson's personal popularity sank lower and lower. On March 31, Johnson again took to the airwaves to address Americans through television and radio about the course of the war in Vietnam.

The message that those listening to Johnson's famous broadcast heard stunned the nation. First, Johnson explained that he was immediately going to begin drawing down American military forces in Vietnam. "We are reducing —substantially reducing—the present level of hostilities," he declared. "And we are doing so unilaterally, and at once." Far more startling to listeners was Johnson's announcement about his own political future. It would not be right, Johnson noted, at a time when the nation was engaged in such a war, for the commander in chief to be occupied with anything other than being president. "Accordingly," he explained, "I shall not seek, and I will not accept, the nomination of my party for another term as your President." The career of one of the most forceful individuals ever to sit in the Oval Office had been cut short by the disastrous conflict in Vietnam.

Good evening, my fellow Americans:
Tonight I want to speak to you of peace in Vietnam and Southeast Asia.

No other question so preoccupies our people. No other dream so absorbs the 250 million human beings who live in that part of the world. No other goal motivates American policy in Southeast Asia.

For years, representatives of our Government and others have traveled the world—seeking to find a basis for peace talks.

Since last September [1967], they have carried the offer that I made public at San Antonio. That offer was this:

That the United States would stop its bombardment of North Vietnam when that would lead promptly to productive discussions—and that we would assume that North Vietnam would not take military advantage of our restraint.

Hanoi denounced this offer, both privately and publicly. Even while the search for peace was going on, North Vietnam rushed their preparations for a savage assault on the people, the government, and the allies of South Vietnam.

The Tet Offensive Failed

Their attack—during the Tet holidays [January 1968]—failed to achieve its principal objectives.

It did not collapse the elected government of South Vietnam or shatter its army—as the Communists had hoped.

It did not produce a "general uprising" among the people of the cities as they had predicted.

The Communists were unable to maintain control of any of the more than 30 cities that they attacked. And they took very heavy casualties.

But they did compel the South Vietnamese and their allies to move certain forces from the countryside into the cities.

They caused widespread disruption and suffering. Their attacks, and the battles that followed, made refugees of half a million human beings.

The Communists may renew their attack any day.

They are, it appears, trying to make 1968 the year of decision in South Vietnam—the year that brings, if not final victory or defeat, at least a turning point in the struggle. This much is clear:

If they do mount another round of heavy attacks, they will not succeed in destroying the fighting power of South Vietnam and its allies.

But tragically, this is also clear: Many men—on both sides of the struggle—will be lost. A nation that has already suffered 20 years of warfare will suffer once again. Armies on both sides will take new casualties. And the war will go on.

There is no need for this to be so.

There is no need to delay the talks that could bring an end to this long and this bloody war.

A Renewed Offer of Peace

Tonight, I renew the offer I made last August—to stop the bombardment of North Vietnam. We ask that talks begin promptly, that they be serious talks on the substance of peace. We assume that during those talks Hanoi will not take advantage of our restraint.

We are prepared to move immediately toward peace through negotiations.

So, tonight, in the hope that this action will lead to early talks, I am taking the first step to deescalate the conflict. We are reducing—substantially reducing—the present level of hostilities.

And we are doing so unilaterally, and at once.

Tonight, I have ordered our aircraft and our naval vessels to make no attacks on North Vietnam, except in the area north of the demilitarized zone where the continuing enemy buildup directly threatens allied forward positions and where the movements of their troops and supplies are clearly related to that threat.

The area in which we are stopping our attacks includes almost 90 percent of North Vietnam's population, and most of its territory. Thus there will be no attacks around the principal populated areas, or in the food-producing areas of North Vietnam.

Even this very limited bombing of the North could come to an early end—if our restraint is matched by restraint in Hanoi. But I cannot in good conscience stop all bombing so long as to do so would immediately and directly endanger the lives of our men and our allies. Whether a complete bombing halt becomes possible in the future will be determined by events.

Our purpose in this action is to bring about a reduction in the level of violence that now exists.

It is to save the lives of brave men—and to save the lives of innocent women and children. It is to permit the contending forces to move closer to a political settlement.

And tonight, I call upon the United Kingdom and I call upon the Soviet Union—as cochairmen of the Geneva Conferences, and as permanent members of the United Nations Security Council—to do all they can to move from the unilateral act of deescalation that I have just announced toward genuine peace in Southeast Asia.

Now, as in the past, the United States is ready to send its representatives to any forum, at any time, to discuss the means of bringing this ugly war to an end.

I am designating one of our most distinguished Americans, Ambassador Averell Harriman, as my personal representative for such talks. In addition, I have asked Ambassador Llewellyn Thompson, who returned from Moscow for consultation, to be available to join Ambassador Harriman at Geneva or any other suitable place—just as soon as Hanoi agrees to a conference.

I call upon President Ho Chi Minh to respond positively, and favorably, to this new step toward peace.

Our Common Strength Is Invincible

But if peace does not come now through negotiations, it will come when Hanoi understands that our common resolve is unshakable, and our common strength is invincible.

Tonight, we and the other allied nations are contributing 600,000 fighting men to assist 700,000 South Vietnamese troops in defending their little country.

Our presence there has always rested on this basic belief: The main burden of preserving their freedom must be carried out by them—by the South Vietnamese themselves.

We and our allies can only help to provide a shield behind which the people of South Vietnam can survive and can grow and develop. On their efforts—on their determination and resourcefulness—the outcome will ultimately depend.

That small, beleaguered nation has suffered terrible punishment for more than 20 years.

I pay tribute once again tonight to the great courage and endurance of its people. South Vietnam supports armed forces tonight of almost 700,000 men—and I call your attention to the fact that this is the equivalent of more than 10 million in our own population. Its people maintain their firm determination to be free of domination by the North. . . .

We applaud this evidence of determination on the part of South Vietnam. Our first priority will be to support their effort.

We shall accelerate the reequipment of South Vietnam's armed forces—in order to meet the enemy's increased firepower. This will enable them progressively to undertake a larger share of combat operations against the Communist invaders.

On many occasions I have told the American people that we would send to Vietnam those forces that are required to accomplish our mission there. So, with that as our guide, we have previously authorized a force level of approximately 525,000.

Some weeks ago—to help meet the enemy's new offensive—we sent to Vietnam about 11,000 additional Marine and airborne troops. They were deployed by air in 48 hours, on an emergency basis. But the artillery, tank, aircraft, medical, and other units that were needed to work with and to support these infantry troops in combat could not then accompany them by air on that short notice.

In order that these forces may reach maximum combat effectiveness, the Joint Chiefs of Staff have recommended to me that we should prepare to send—during the next 5 months—support troops totaling approximately 13,500 men.

A portion of these men will be made available from our active forces. The balance will come from reserve component units which will be called up for service.

One Day There Will Be Peace

One day, my fellow citizens, there will be peace in Southeast Asia.

It will come because the people of Southeast Asia want it—those whose armies are at war tonight, and those who, though threatened, have thus far been spared.

Peace will come because Asians were willing to work for it-and to sacrifice for it—and to die by the thousands for it.

But let it never be forgotten: Peace will come also because America sent her sons to help secure it.

It has not been easy—far from it. During the past 4½ years, it has been my fate and my responsibility to be Commander in Chief. I have lived—daily and nightly—with the cost of this war. I know the pain that it has inflicted. I know, perhaps better than anyone, the misgivings that it has aroused.

Throughout this entire, long period, I have been sustained by a single principle: that what we are doing now, in Vietnam, is vital not only to the security of Southeast Asia, but it is vital to the security of every American.

Surely we have treaties which we must respect. Surely we have commitments that we are going to keep. Resolutions of the Congress testify to the need to resist aggression in the world and in Southeast Asia.

But the heart of our involvement in South Vietnam—under three different presidents, three separate administrations—has always been America's own security.

And the larger purpose of our involvement has always been to help the nations of Southeast Asia become independent and stand alone, self-sustaining, as members of a great world community—at peace with themselves, and at peace with all others.

With such an Asia, our country—and the world—will be far more secure than it is tonight.

I believe that a peaceful Asia is far nearer to reality because of what America has done in Vietnam. I believe that the men who endure the dangers of battle—fighting there for us tonight —are helping the entire world avoid far greater conflicts, far wider wars, far more destruction, than this one.

The peace that will bring them home someday will come. Tonight I have offered the first in what I hope will be a series of mutual moves toward peace.

I pray that it will not be rejected by the leaders of North Vietnam. I pray that they will accept it as a means by which the sacrifices of their own people may be ended. And I ask your help and your support, my fellow citizens, for this effort to reach across the battlefield toward an early peace.

Finally, my fellow Americans, let me say this:

Of those to whom much is given, much is asked. I cannot say and no man could say that no more will be asked of us.

Yet, I believe that now, no less than when the decade began, this generation of Americans is willing to "pay any price, bear any burden, meet any hardship, support any friend, oppose any foe to assure the survival and the success of liberty."

Since those words were spoken by John F. Kennedy, the people of America have kept that compact with mankind's noblest cause.

And we shall continue to keep it.

Yet, I believe that we must always be mindful of this one thing, whatever the trials and the tests ahead. The ultimate strength of our country and our cause will lie not in powerful weapons or infinite resources or boundless wealth, but will lie in the unity of our people.

This I believe very deeply.

There Is Division in America

Throughout my entire public career I have followed the personal philosophy that I am a free man, an American, a public servant, and a member of my party, in that order always and only.

For 37 years in the service of our Nation, first as a Congressman, as a Senator, and as Vice President, and now as your President, I have put the unity of the people first. I have put it ahead of any divisive partisanship.

And in these times as in times before, it is true that a house divided against itself by the spirit of faction, of party, of region, of religion, of race, is a house that cannot stand.

There is division in the American house now. There is divisiveness among us all tonight. And holding the trust that is mine, as President of all the people, I cannot disregard the peril to the progress of the American people and the hope and the prospect of peace for all peoples.

So, I would ask all Americans, whatever their personal interests or concern, to guard against divisiveness and all its ugly consequences.

Fifty-two months and 10 days ago, in a moment of tragedy and trauma, the duties of this office fell upon me. I asked then for your help and God's, that we might continue America on its course, binding up our wounds, healing our history, moving forward in new unity, to clear the American agenda and to keep the American commitment for all of our people.

United we have kept that commitment. United we have enlarged that commitment.

Through all time to come, I think America will be a stronger nation, a more just society, and a land of greater opportunity and fulfillment because of what we have all done together in these years of unparalleled achievement.

Our reward will come in the life of freedom, peace, and hope that our children will enjoy through ages ahead.

What we won when all of our people united just must not now be lost in suspicion, distrust, selfishness, and politics among any of our people.

I Shall Not Seek Nomination

Believing this as I do, I have concluded that I should not permit the Presidency to become involved in the partisan divisions that are developing in this political year.

With America's sons in the fields far away, with America's future under challenge right here at home, with our hopes and the world's hopes for peace in the balance every day, I do not believe that I should devote an hour or a day of my time to any personal partisan causes or to any duties other than the awesome duties of this office—the Presidency of your country.

Accordingly, I shall not seek, and I will not accept, the nomination of my party for another term as your President.

But let men everywhere know, however, that a strong, a confident, and a vigilant America stands ready tonight to seek an honorable peace—and stands ready tonight to defend an honored cause—whatever the price, whatever the burden, whatever the sacrifice that duty may require.

Thank you for listening. Good night and God bless all of you.

Reaching Peace with Honor

Richard Milhous Nixon

In January 1973 (the day after Lyndon Baines Johnson died in Texas of a heart attack) President Richard Milhous Nixon made a radio and television broadcast to the nation in which he announced that the United States and North Vietnam had signed an agreement "to end the war and bring peace with honor in Vietnam and Southeast Asia." The announcement had a galvanizing effect upon the American audience at home: The Vietnam conflict had been the single most important issue in American politics and American society for almost a decade, and suddenly it was over. During the era literally millions of Americans had served in the U.S. military; hundreds of thousands more had faced the prospect of being drafted and perhaps dying in Southeast Asia. Opposition to the war had been one of the foundational beliefs of both "flower-child" hippies and militant extremists (or terrorists) such as the Weatherman Underground, while support for the war had been an important point for American anti-Communists. Millions of Americans, divided about the war, found themselves holding opinions that fell between these two points of view, and discussed and argued the topic accordingly. Vietnam was the overwhelming and inescapable question of the period.

In this address, Nixon thanked the South Vietnamese for their efforts and announced that the United States would continue to provide material—though not military—

Richard Milhous Nixon, address to the nation, Washington, DC, January 23, 1973.

support to South Vietnam in its struggle with the North. Through their courage, he explained, the South Vietnamese had earned the right to self-determination; in other words, the U.S. military would not be able to provide help any longer. Nixon then thanked Americans for their perseverance through the conflict and noted that Americans should be proud that the United States had not settled for an agreement that "would have betrayed our allies." Despite his attempts to portray the peace as an American and South Vietnamese victory, it was clear to the millions of Americans listening to Nixon's 1973 broadcast that the United States had, for the first time in history, essentially lost a military conflict. Whether they were relieved to hear about the end of the war or were shamed by that defeat (or both), those listening were aware that with this address a significant period in U.S. history was coming closer to an end.

Good evening:
I have asked for this radio and television time tonight for the purpose of announcing that we today have concluded an agreement to end the war and bring peace with honor in Vietnam and in Southeast Asia.

The following statement is being issued at this moment in Washington and Hanoi:

At 12:30 Paris time today, January 23, 1973, the Agreement on Ending the War and Restoring Peace in Vietnam was initialed by [U.S. national security adviser] Dr. Henry Kissinger on behalf of the United States, and Special Adviser Le Duc Tho on behalf of the Democratic Republic of Vietnam.

The agreement will be formally signed by the parties participating in the Paris Conference on Vietnam on January 27, 1973, at the International Conference Center in Paris.

The cease-fire will take effect at 2400 Greenwich Mean Time, January 27, 1973. The United States and the Democratic Republic of Vietnam express the hope that this agreement will insure stable peace in Vietnam and contribute to the preservation of lasting peace in Indochina and Southeast Asia.

What Is "Peace with Honor"?

That concludes the formal statement. Throughout the years of negotiations, we have insisted on peace with honor. In my addresses to the Nation from this room of January 25 and May 8 [1972], I set forth the goals that we considered essential for peace with honor.

In the settlement that has now been agreed to, all the conditions that I laid down then have been met:

A cease-fire, internationally supervised, will begin at 7 P.M., this Saturday, January 27, Washington time.

Within 60 days from this Saturday, all Americans held prisoners of war throughout Indochina will be released. There will be the fullest possible accounting for all of those who are missing in action.

During the same 60-day period, all American forces will be withdrawn from South Vietnam.

The people of South Vietnam have been guaranteed the right to determine their own future, without outside interference.

By joint agreement, the full text of the agreement and the protocol to carry it out will be issued tomorrow.

Throughout these negotiations we have been in the closest consultation with President Thieu and other representatives of the Republic of Vietnam. This settlement meets the goals and has the full support of President Thieu and the Government of the Republic of Vietnam, as well as that of our other allies who are affected.

The United States will continue to recognize the Government of the Republic of Vietnam as the sole legitimate government of South Vietnam.

We shall continue to aid South Vietnam within the terms of the agreement, and we shall support efforts by the people of South Vietnam to settle their problems peacefully among themselves.

We must recognize that ending the war is only the first step toward building the peace. All parties must now see to it that this is a peace that lasts, and also a peace that heals—and a peace that not only ends the war in Southeast Asia but contributes to the prospects of peace in the whole world.

This will mean that the terms of the agreement must be scrupulously adhered to. We shall do everything the agreement requires of us, and we shall expect the other parties to do everything it requires of them. We shall also expect other interested nations to help insure that the agreement is carried out and peace is maintained.

Words to the Parties in the Conflict

As this long and very difficult war ends, I would like to address a few special words to each of those who have been parties in the conflict.

First, to the people and Government of South Vietnam: By your courage, by your sacrifice, you have won the precious right to determine your own future, and you have developed the strength to defend that right. We look forward to working with you in the future—friends in peace as we have been allies in war.

To the leaders of North Vietnam: As we have ended the war through negotiations, let us now build a peace of reconciliation. For our part, we are prepared to make a major effort to help achieve that goal. But just as reciprocity was needed to end the war, so too will it be needed to build and strengthen the peace.

To the other major powers that have been involved even indirectly: Now is the time for mutual restraint so that the peace we have achieved can last.

And finally, to all of you who are listening, the American people: Your steadfastness in supporting our insistence on peace with honor has made peace with honor possible. I know that you would not have wanted that peace jeopardized. With our secret negotiations at the sensitive stage they were in during this recent period, for me to have discussed publicly our efforts to secure peace would not only have violated our understanding with North Vietnam, it would have seriously harmed and possibly destroyed the chances for peace. Therefore, I know that you now can understand why, during these past several weeks, I have not made any public statements about those efforts.

Getting the Right Kind of Peace

The important thing was not to talk about peace, but to get peace—and to get the right kind of peace. This we have done.

Now that we have achieved an honorable agreement, let us be proud that America did not settle for a peace that would have betrayed our allies, that would have abandoned our prisoners of war, or that would have ended the war for us but would have continued the war for the 50 million people of Indochina. Let us be proud of the 2½ million young Americans who served in Vietnam, who served with honor and distinction in one of the most selfless enterprises in the history of nations. And let us be proud of those who sacrificed, who gave their lives so that the people of South Vietnam might live in freedom and so that the world might live in peace.

In particular, I would like to say a word to some of the bravest people I have ever met—the wives, the children, the families of our prisoners of war and the missing in action. When others called on us to settle on any terms, you had the courage to stand for the right kind of peace so that those who died and those who suffered would not have died and suffered in vain, and so that where this generation knew war, the next generation would know peace. Nothing means more to me at this moment than the fact that your long vigil is coming to an end.

Just yesterday, a great American, who once occupied this office, died. In his life, President Johnson endured the vilification of those who sought to portray him as a man of war. But there was nothing he cared about more deeply than achieving a lasting peace in the world.

I remember the last time I talked with him. It was just the day after New Year's. He spoke then of his concern with bringing peace, with making it the right kind of peace, and I was grateful that he once again expressed his support for my efforts to gain such a peace. No one would have welcomed this peace more than he.

And I know he would join me in asking—for those who died and for those who live—let us consecrate this moment by resolving together to make the peace we have achieved a peace that will last. Thank you and good evening.

CHAPTER 2

Protesting American Involvement in Vietnam

 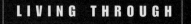

Refusing to Be Drafted

Donald L. Simons

Americans who became adults during the Vietnam era faced the frightening possibility of being drafted into the military and sent into combat in Vietnam. While many Americans supported the war itself, and some were eager to get into uniform, in general America's youths were desperately anxious about the possibility of being sent to fight in the jungles of Southeast Asia. Still, most Americans who were subject to the draft either accepted induction into the military or else sought legal means to avoid service in Vietnam (by entering college or by serving with the Coast Guard or the National Guard). Still, all Americans knew or had heard of someone who had done everything possible to avoid the draft, including perhaps fleeing the country. According to some estimates, there were approximately 570,000 draft offenders. Of this number only 25,000 were actually indicted and only 4,000 were ever imprisoned.

In this excerpt, Donald L. Simons, a young student who believed that any killing was wrong and who therefore sought conscientious objector (CO) status, describes how he formally refused induction into the military after his request for CO status was denied. Simons initially sought a medical exemption, but after several encounters with military officials he abandoned this approach and simply refused to be drafted. Simons viewed the process of his refusing induction wryly; in describing his encounters with career military men at the induction center he concludes that he and they came from two entirely different worlds, and that they would never be able to understand each other.

After refusing induction into the U.S. Army, Simons fought his induction in court, but eventually lost the legal battle. Still refusing to be drafted, Simons fled to Canada, where he remained for five years before President Gerald Ford's blanket pardon of all draft offenders enabled him to return to the United States. *I Refuse: Memories of a Vietnam War Objector*, his account of his effort to avoid the draft, was published in 1992.

The draft board office was located on the third floor of a faded, yellow brick building with metal windows and venetian blinds. Armed Forces recruiters shared the floor, their crackerbox offices vying for visitors' attention as one walked the narrow hallway to the last door on the right.

I had dealt face-to-face with the draft board clerk on several occasions, a bland woman who replaced an old lady whose retirement had long been overdue. Though they had no real legal authority, these clerks wielded considerable influence; actually, they made most of the day-to-day decisions. The results were then approved by the board members, who often met only once a month.

I would say this clerk and I were friends inasmuch as she had expressed concern for me a time or two. Violating draft law led to a great deal of legal trouble, and even prison, she reminded me, not without her bias.

"I don't know what you people are trying to do," I declared walking in the door. "What's this new induction order for November 3rd? Why do you keep sending me induction orders when you know my position?"

She put on her best cool, defensive face.

"It's regulations, Mr. Simons. For all we know, you want to challenge the draft law in court. There are established procedures for that, and we have to get our part right. As for your failing to appear for induction on October 6th, you didn't tell us what happened. We have had inductees oversleep, you know."

"Oversleep?"

Her face softened.

"We also have young men who, like you, have filed for CO status, and not succeeding, have changed their minds."

"My mind is made up."

"But you've got to be present on the induction date," she said standing. "You can refuse at the appropriate time in the proceedings, but you must go through the initial phase. That's why we gave you a new induction date."

I did not believe her. I sensed the plan was to get me there, then to either intimidate me into complying, or to induct me before I knew what happened.

"If you intend a court challenge," she continued, "then sooner or later you will have to be present at an induction date. Litigation cannot begin until the Selective Service part of it is concluded."

This was totally absurd; I could not believe it. I was telling them they could take their induction order and stick it, and they were saying okay, but it had to be done according to rules and regulations.

On the other hand, I noted how she kept mentioning court and litigation, no doubt suspecting I was nervous about the prospect. And she was right. She was more than right; I could hear the confidence in her voice. She knew from experience that the chances were slim for a draft case succeeding in court if it was not resolved by the Selective Service System; in theory, a registrant was given every opportunity to make his case without having to resort to the courts. In reality though, it did not necessarily work that way, and I was living proof.

I had nothing else to say to the clerk beyond shaking my head, and storming back down the hall. Why did I get the impression she was enjoying this? Her eyes said, "Simons, the poor little college student. He should grow up, be more like a man, like the guys from the mines and the farms; they didn't make such a fuss." . . .

Instructions

Our thorough and efficient local board clerk was also there [on November 3] checking off the names of the draftees as we arrived.

"Good morning," I said leaning toward her. "I'm not staying. I just wanted you to see for the record that I did show up for an induction date."

She looked pleased, but anxious to correct me. "Oh, but you can't go just yet. You must stay long enough to get instructions."

"Instructions?" I said. "For what? I'm not being inducted."

"Please have a seat, Mr. Simons. You'll understand more in a few minutes." With suddenly mounting anxiety, I sat by myself at a table near the front door.

The room reminded me of a cafeteria, with heavy metal, pedestaled tables and lightly cushioned, armless metal chairs. The gray formica table tops were sticky from the complimentary coffee. . . .

The clerk and the director of the local Red Cross moved to the front tables to give instructions and to offer inspiration. To their left, a large American flag stood militarily, as three other inductees, in the first row, looked on with anticipation. . . .

The "instructions" the clerk referred to was her first order of business; she advised everyone how to get to the induction center in the neighboring town, should anyone wish to go by car rather than in the bus provided. To my dismay I found out that I would have to go to the induction center to formally register my refusal to be inducted. With no further need for me to be there I left, shuddering in disgust as the director of the local Red Cross began cooing his inspirational remarks.

Thou Shalt Kill

For most people this process began harmlessly enough, or so it seemed, with the words on the induction notice, "You are hereby ordered to report. . . ." But this was only the beginning of the ordering. Once in the army it would be all orders, commands one was bound to obey, right to the order to kill, which one's survival instincts would have him do, and do many times over regardless of the psychological and spiritual consequences.

"Thou shalt not kill," our religions taught, though our governments contend thou shalt kill under certain political circumstances. One had better follow the government's line or there was the threat of prosecution and prison. For most, that threat canceled the moral choice.

For instance, a friend asked with concern if I was aware that refusing induction was a federal offense, and that I could be imprisoned, as if that was what was important, not the nation's blindness to the moral catastrophe which was the continuing war.

Perhaps this friend's myopia helped to keep him from feeling the guilt this war generated in all of us. Some, like veterans of previous wars, found their way around it by an excess of patriotism, by embracing the government which had also given them the license to kill. The hawk veterans organizations were a case in point, members of the "my country, love it or leave it" crowd. Of course, should one leave, he would not be welcomed back; because those that did leave symbolized the nation's moral failing, something that even the hawks felt beneath their flags, ribbons, and medals. To get around this, some hawks went on to become members of local draft boards, believing wrongly that by ushering others to war they would not feel so bad.

The saddest consequence of this was the perpetuation of an attitude where the military and war were seen as something good. Accordingly, draftees were treated to these send-off ceremonies with a hardy handshake, a pat on the back, and assurances they were doing the right thing for God and country. In fact it was the wrong thing; the truth is, humans killing humans is a moral offense of the highest magnitude, and no government has the right to order it. . . .

A Set-Up?

The induction center in the neighboring town was not the one I was previously sent to for my pre-induction physical exam. Checking the address, I drove through the neighborhood twice before finally spotting it. As my heart pounded anxiously, I pulled into the parking lot and tried to calm myself; after all, I was probably only there for a simple matter, like signing a form to refuse induction.

Out of the car, I marched through the two sets of glass doors, across the narrow lobby, and to an enlisted man at the front desk.

"May I help you?" he asked.

"I'm from Morgantown, and was supposed to be inducted today, but I want to refuse. Can you tell me how to go about doing that?"

He stared at me a moment, stunned; he looked down, then back up again. "I'll be right back. Have a seat."

I crossed the room to a row of well-worn chairs, but because I was nervous, chose not to sit. Instead I went back to the glass doors, where I saw it was beginning to snow.

Returning, the enlisted man informed me that before I could refuse, I would have to take the induction physical exam.

"You must be kidding," I said.

"Those are regulations."

Suddenly the whole picture flashed before me: the local board clerk said I had to be present on the induction date; then I was told I had to go to the induction center; now I had to take the physical exam. It was a set-up after all. They planned to induct me.

"Those men over there are going in for the physical in a few minutes," said the enlisted man. "You can go with them."

Undermining Individuality

I said nothing, returning to the glass doors to rethink the situation. There was nothing to keep me from walking out again, I reminded myself, though I also wondered if I was not making more of this than there really was; perhaps I was just being paranoid. The Selective Service and the military could not trick someone, could not induct a guy without his knowing it. That would be illegal. On the other hand, had they not gotten me this far? After all, here I was standing in the induction center.

Just inside the physical examination room was a changing area, but with no lockers or benches. There was, however, an L-shaped shelf across the end wall and down one side, where clothes could be stashed in individual mounds. Stripped to my shorts, it was a matter of going from station to station, assembly line style, being weighed, having eyes checked, ears inspected, and so on down the anatomy. I was fortunate to be in a small group this time, unlike the previous physical which was truly a cattle drive.

Expediency, I supposed, was the principal reason for the group approach, though the psychological effect was surely part of it. The purpose was to undermine individuality. An army needed homogeneity more than individuality. Which was not to say the medical staff was overbearing; they were good-natured and went about their routine as though it was merely a job. Indeed, some of the inductees looked admiringly on these staffers, impressed by their emblems and stripes. That too was part of the psychology, I was sure. I saw this before, in high school, when the local recruiters came to dazzle the guys. It was pure deception, then and now, an attempt to mask what a soldier really was, what an army really did. Sadly, those impressed young men who were with me in that induction center assembly line would discover the truth soon enough.

Attempting to Be Declared Unfit

With the completion of the physical exam, I was directed to an office down the hall, the office of the head medical officer. Inside, I sat uncomfortably on a metal chair by the door, my bare feet fidgeting on the spotless, cold tile floor. Presently then, in strode a tall, hefty Marine Corps captain-physician; he greeted me with a thick Southern accent.

"I've read this letter from your doctor," he said, flashing the page in his hand. "Tell me, how do you feel right now?"

"Not too bad," I said uncertainly, if not caught by surprise.

"Can you describe your symptoms for this problem of yours," he asked as he plopped down and leaned back in his big chair.

That I was being asked for the symptoms struck me as quite funny, though I dared not crack a smile. The doctor in Pittsburgh had urged me to study the symptoms he had outlined, so if asked I would sound convincing. I failed to review them, an indication of my lack of commitment to this approach.

"Well," I said, trying my best, "my heart skips beats under stress. . . ."

Hooking on his stethoscope, the officer rose and began checking here and there around my heart. After several minutes, he returned to his desk, pondered briefly, only to pick up the telephone. Dialing, he again tilted back in his chair, as I looked on in bewilderment.

When the person on the other end answered, the captain stated cordially that he had a young man there at the Armed Forces Induction Center, who had a letter from that office. I closed my eyes. But when I opened them again, I discovered the officer still talking to the "good doctor," who said he recalled my case, that he had observed thus and so, and that in his opinion I was not fit for military service. A smile of appreciation came to my face; he could just as easily have denied knowing me. Following some technical talk, the captain hung up.

But alas, it was for naught. Rather, it was now one for, and one against disqualification. A third opinion was needed, and for that I would have to go over to the local hospital, though I preferred to forget about the whole thing.

"It's late afternoon," said the officer, his Southern drawl rising. "You can make the hospital today, but you'll have to come back here tomorrow to finish your processing."

Nodding, I thanked him, I was not sure why, and departed. Mostly though, I was annoyed because I knew what the third opinion would be, and were it not for my playing this game, I probably would have had the refusal of induction papers signed by then.

But, it appeared fate had other things in mind for me, who knew the dynamics of it? Quite possibly there was some unfinished spiritual business being worked out here, business requiring more than a doctor's letter.

Back at the Induction Center

It was a bright, sunny, cold morning as I again drove the 20 miles to the induction center, with the knowledge this day was going to be quite different. For one, there would be no VFW send-off ceremony, and no more physical exams; only refusing induction remained.

Back through the two sets of glass doors, I once again stepped to the counter, except the enlisted man there was different from the day before. My words, however, were the same. I was there to refuse induction. Giving him my name, I said I had already been through most of the processing, if he could just tell me how I was to refuse. As startled as the first man, he too disappeared into the next room to find out.

Meanwhile, I overheard two of the staff talking in the hall ahead; they were laughing about the threats of disruption the center had received the day before, some students in Morgantown, including a draftee, planning an assault. They noted with some satisfaction that it had not materialized. . . .

Before long, the enlisted man reappeared with a sergeant. In his early fifties and impressively uniformed with medals, buttons, ribbons and stripes, the sergeant was undoubtedly a "lifer." I suspected that, years ago, he could not wait to enlist on his eighteenth birthday. A lean man, five feet ten, and with a crew cut and a drill sergeant's demeanor, he directed me to his desk in a room off the hall to the right. That morning though, there were few others in the room making our business intimate and all the more uncomfortable.

Was it loathing which kept the sergeant's words to a minimum as he filled out papers for the refusal? He did not look at me the whole time; then again, I did not look at him either. We knew we were from different planets.

After I signed the papers, we went to the office of a lieutenant, a psychologist as it turned out. A man not much older than me, he looked to be a graduate of the Reserve Officer Training Corps. Clean cut and wholesome, he brought back memories of compulsory ROTC when I was a freshman and sophomore. For most of us, it was something between an inconvenience and a joke, those going into the advanced program considered weird.

Initially, we liked ROTC because of the uniforms, everyone curious to see what he looked like in one. I thought I looked pretty good, as I was sure the others did. Doing this fulfilled the soldier fantasy we all had as little boys in our militarized society.

Typical of American parents of the time, my father and mother fed into it; when I put on the ROTC uniform, my father saluted, and my mother looked on proudly. But to me, it was only a fantasy, an illusion. Consequently, it scared me when I discovered some of the other guys taking it very, very seriously.

Doing What Must Be Done

But now then, what was I to make of this lieutenant? He seemed harmless enough, and in his mild manner he simply asked why I wanted to refuse. I went on to explain about my conscientious objection, albeit after five minutes it was apparent he was not really interested; he only wanted to see whether I was crazy or on drugs. As I was neither, he signed his part of the papers, and directed me to another office where I was left alone for some time.

There were no lights on in the room, only a modest few rays of daylight filtering through mostly closed venetian blinds. . . . I was suddenly feeling quite chilly. Just then though, in walked another officer, a captain, his round, honest-looking face making you want him as your bookkeeper. He turned out to be the commander of the induction center, although he seemed a bit young for that.

"Hello," I said, not sure whether I should stand.

As he set my paperwork on his desk and sat down he said, "I'm not here to talk you out of doing this. I'm sure you've given it a great deal of thought. Simply, it is my duty to inform you that refusing induction is a federal offense. I am required to report your refusal to the Selective Service, who in turn will report it to the Justice Department for prosecution. You do understand that, don't you?"

"Yes," I said looking up. "You have to do what you have to do, just as I am doing what I have to do."

As I watched him sign his part of the papers, I was struck by the incongruity—here was this very courteous, pleasant person, a nice guy, signing papers he knew would probably send me to prison. How could I not feel sad as I watched his pen cross the page, much as I felt sad at the lieutenant's and the sergeant's signings. Again the word "illusion" came to mind;

with their uniforms, ranks, commands, procedures and jargon there was something unreal about the military. Then again, I supposed they had to have those things in order to do what they did: wage war, kill people and send those who refused to cooperate off to jail.

The plush, narrow ceremony room, designed as it was for three rows of inductees, had a low stage at the front where stood the captain, the lieutenant, and the sergeant. I stood where I assumed I was to be, choosing the inconspicuous last position in the back row; I did not intend, nor was it in my personality to make a scene, though I noticed the trio keeping a steady eye on me. I wondered, as I looked at all the other young men, whether the three on the stage assumed that with the psychological pressure of the setting and the group, I would relent. I believed the draft board and these three thought I would. Probably in the past, some like me had. On the other hand, I could not help but feel that this scene was rare; West Virginia was not known for draft resistance. In that way, I felt oddly proud as one of the few: ". . . one of the few, the proud," but not a Marine.

I Was a Proud Felon

The captain explained we were about to enter military service, that he would say the words "United States Army," following which everyone would say his name, and step forward; doing so constituted induction. I reminded myself it was not too late, that I could save myself enormous trouble by just taking that one step. Everyone would understand; no one would hold it against me. Submitting was the norm. In fact, there were those, including some in my own family who would feel relieved. In their eyes, by taking that step I would prove to be a "patriot" after all. I would be no different than them, given their own reservations about the killing in Vietnam. And like them, I would have concluded that the government knew more about the situation over there, and was doing what was right. For them, it would be the loyal thing to do to submit.

These thoughts were all well and good except for one thing, they were not true. I was not like everybody else; I did not believe what the government was doing was right, anymore than I believed that blind loyalty was a good enough reason to allow oneself to be inducted into an organization that killed people. Indeed if there was loyalty to be had, it was me to my conscience.

Just then I heard the captain's words, "United States Army," followed by all the voices, and the single clump forward. My mouth moved with all the others, but it was not my name I said. "I refuse," were my words, my feet remaining firmly planted.

Just as everyone looked to see why I had not moved, the sergeant barked, "Left face!" Some of the farm boys, those who had not had the benefit of compulsory ROTC, turned only their heads to the left, rather than their whole bodies. It would be the last time they made that mistake.

But soon they were organized and marching to the lead of the sergeant, leaving me alone still facing the captain, and the lieutenant. But it was done now, wasn't it? There was nothing left for anyone to say. Walking past me, the captain said I was free to go; the lieutenant, meanwhile, smiled in apparent amazement.

The act itself was simple enough; indeed, the whole affair took less than 40 minutes. To say I was a proud felon would be close to it, proud of myself for seeing it through. But mostly, I was a satisfied felon. I had denied the war its fuel, albeit one drop; if it continued to rage, I knew it was not because of me. Its perpetuation was the doing of the captain, lieutenant, sergeant, the draft board, and all the others in our society who blindly followed the government line. And those who did not? For my part, I now felt in a different league; I had just earned my first stripe.

The Demonstration at the 1968 Chicago Convention

Fred Halstead

The 1968 Chicago Democratic National Convention was the site of two of the most important and well-publicized events of the Vietnam era: first, the Democratic nomination of Vice President Hubert Humphrey to run for president of the United States, and second (and more importantly) the mass antiwar protests by the National Mobilizing Committee to End the War in Vietnam (Mobe) and the accompanying police riot. The police violence against the protesters was televised live to the nation and convinced many Americans that the Democrats were unable to maintain order without brutality. The national convention thus contributed to Humphrey's defeat by Richard Nixon in the November election.

In this article, Fred Halstead, a committed Socialist, member of the Socialist Workers Party, and the party's candidate for president of the United States in the 1968 election, describes the events surrounding the Chicago national convention. As an important participant in the movement against the Vietnam War he was intimately familiar with the events of the period and with such antiwar leaders as Tom Hayden of the Students for a Democratic Society (SDS) and Abbie Hoffman of the Youth International Party (Yippies). While Halstead worked alongside such leaders, however, and they all shared the common goal of ending the war in Vietnam, there were serious tensions between these leaders and their organizations. The Socialist Workers Party did not attend or participate in the rally in any way. Nevertheless, his account reveals how members of the antiwar community viewed the events in Chicago, and how by 1968 American society was fracturing along political lines. Fred Halstead is the author of *Out Now! A Participant's Account of the American Movement Against the Vietnam War* (1978).

As the demonstrations approached, the moderate groups, as well as some of the pacifists, took their distance from the actions. What is more, the McCarthy campaign canceled most of its own plans for activities outside the convention, and [Minnesota senator and Democratic candidate Eugene] McCarthy himself appealed for his followers not to come to Chicago for demonstrations.

One reason for this may have been that the McCarthy campaign had gotten wind of how Chicago's Mayor Richard Daley —a key figure in the Democratic Party and a strong Humphrey backer—intended to deal with the demonstrators.

Consequently, the turnout for the demonstrations was far smaller than anyone had predicted, perhaps 15,000 all told, and only some 10,000 on hand for the largest single gathering. This was in the face of the fact that beforehand the Mobe [National Mobilization Committee to End the War in Vietnam] announced it was making housing arrangements for 50,000 and printing up 100,000 copies of a demonstrators' guide, while the Mobe applications for permits had estimated 150,000.

On Sunday, August 25, the day before the convention opened, a rally of 5,000 youthful supporters welcomed McCarthy to town. This rally was not sponsored by the Mobe and the only mention of opposition to the war at this affair was in several thousand leaflets distributed by the SMC [Student Mobilization Committee], advertising one of its meetings. The same day there was the first of a series of workshops and movement centers around town called by National Mobe, in which different groups discussed whatever they wanted and made plans

for various street actions. Several of the largest of these workshops took place at Lincoln Park near the Old Town section of
the near north side.

The Yippies had previously announced a camp-in in Lincoln Park as part of their "Festival of Life," but the authorities
had refused a permit. At 11:00 P.M. police announced over
bullhorns the closing of the park. Some 1,500 persons had
gathered there by shortly after midnight when the cops moved
in. The police used tear gas and clubs, and threw people in the
park pond. A number of newsmen were targets of police attack. Gas wafted over into Old Town, an area of cafes and
shops frequented by student-aged youth, while the police
moved through the area roughing up people who looked like
hippies or demonstrators. Taunted by shouts of "pig" and
greeted with occasional missiles, they responded by indiscrimi-
nate clubbings. This scene was repeated Monday night, and
that pretty much set the tone for the rest of the week. According to a later report drawn up by a team of investigators under
the direction of Daniel Walker, then president of the Chicago
Crime Commission, "To read dispassionately the hundreds of
statements describing at first hand the events of Sunday and
Monday nights is to become convinced of the presence of what
can only be called a police riot."

During the daylight hours of Monday and Tuesday there
were several marches, ranging from a few hundred to 1,500
persons or so. Some were peaceful and some involved scuffles
and a few arrests. But they were followed by general police
thumping of youths, including bystanders, in the Old Town
area after dark, as well as sweeps of the park after closing hour.
On Monday and Tuesday night the demonstrators built
makeshift barricades in the park and tried to hold their ground
at least for a time.

None of the demonstrations got anywhere near the Amphitheatre where the convention was being held, which was about four
miles southwest of the Loop at Halsted and Forty-third streets. A
thirty-block area around the Amphitheatre was sealed off by
chain-link fence and police checkpoints. National guardsmen
were encamped in several parks nearby. The city administration

had refused all permits to march to the Amphitheatre. Prefabricated plywood walls were set up along some approaching routes, apparently so the delegates coming from the Loop hotels to the convention couldn't see parts of Chicago's slums.

The First Violence on the Day of the Rally

On Wednesday, August 28, the day of the nomination, some 10,000 demonstrators gathered at a National Mobe rally in the bandshell area of Grant Park, a mile or so south of the center of the Loop. The rally was orderly until a young man lowered the American flag from a flagpole. Some cops moved to arrest him and were heckled by members of the crowd seated in that area. Seizing on this incident, a phalanx of about forty cops waded into that part of the crowd, clubbing freely. People scrambled out of the way, desperately climbing over overturned benches. Some were hurt. Another part of the crowd began to face off at the police.

Rennie Davis [the national coordinator for Mobe], who unlike [Jerry] Rubin [cofounder of the Youth International Party, or Yippies] was inclined to be in the thick of things even after they got sticky, moved with a line of marshals between the crowd and the cops, facing the crowd and trying to get people back in their seats. Some of the cops charged again and Davis was clubbed from behind and knocked unconscious.

At this point it is necessary to set the geographical scene. Grant Park lies between Lake Michigan on the east and Michigan Avenue on the west. Across Michigan Avenue from the park are hotels where many delegates were staying and where convention caucusing was going on. The strip of park directly on Michigan Avenue is separated from the rest—including the bandshell area—by a deep railroad channel which must be crossed by bridges.

[*Liberation* magazine founder David] Dellinger wanted to lead a nonviolent march from the rally across the nearest bridges, then south on Michigan Avenue toward the Amphitheatre. This route would not have taken the marchers directly in front of the convention hotels, since they would have emerged onto Michigan Avenue somewhat south of the hotel area.

He proposed that the crowd divide into two parts: those who were willing to face arrest would march to the Amphitheatre, and those who did not could either go north through the park or disperse. As the march to the Amphitheatre moved west it found the bridges blocked by police and National Guard units, including military vehicles with racks of barbed wire attached to their fronts. Dellinger then started a sit-down.

Confusion About Where to Go

[Founder of the Students for a Democratic Society] Tom Hayden, however, had delivered an impassioned speech to the rally after Davis was knocked out, which was not entirely in line with Dellinger's plan. According to the *Chicago Daily News*, Hayden said:

> This city and the military machinery it has aimed at us won't permit us to protest in an organized fashion.
>
> Therefore we must move out of this park in groups throughout this city and turn this excited, overheated military machine against itself.
>
> Let us make sure that if blood flows, it flows all over the city; if they use gas against us, let's make sure they use gas against their own citizens.
>
> If the police run wild, let them run wild all over Chicago—not just over us sitting in the park. If they are going to disrupt us and our march, let them disrupt the whole city.

Part of the crowd following Dellinger did not sit down. Some of them simply dispersed, especially after tear gas was used. But part of them swung around and joined the group moving north, making about 3,000.

They found each bridge blocked until they reached Monroe Drive, about a mile north, where they swarmed across. By coincidence at just that time a parade of about a hundred Blacks and a mule wagon, led by the Rev. Ralph Abernathy of the Southern Christian Leadership Conference, was coming south on Michigan Avenue. This group had a parade permit and a police escort. The crowd from Grant Park joined in a move south along with the mule wagon toward the hotels on Michigan Avenue.

Then the police made what would appear later as a first-class blunder. Instead of letting the march continue south on Michigan Avenue, at least as far as some more isolated spot, they halted it in front of the Conrad Hilton, one of the main convention hotels, where a lot of McCarthy delegates were staying. Meanwhile another couple of thousand people, not all of them demonstrators, had gathered in the general area of the Hilton. Speakers in the crowd shouted to move on with the march. While TV cameras rolled, the cops waded in with clubs swinging.

Some of the action was later described in the Walker report[1]:

> A part of the crowd was trapped in front of the Conrad Hilton and pressed hard against a big plate-glass window of the Haymarket Lounge. A reporter who was sitting inside said, "Frightened men and women banged . . . against the window, that it might get knocked in. As I backed away a few feet I could see a smudge of blood on the glass outside."
>
> With a sickening crack, the window shattered, and screaming men and women tumbled through, some cut badly by jagged glass. The police came after them.
>
> "I was pushed through by the force of large numbers of people," one victim said. "I got a deep cut on my right leg, diagnosed later as a severed artery. . . . I fell to the floor of the bar. There were 10 to 20 people who had come through. . . . I could not stand on the leg. It was bleeding profusely.
>
> "A squad of policemen burst into the bar, clubbing all those who looked to them like demonstrators."

The report described the beating by police outside the Hilton of a youth who looked about fifteen years old, and then continued:

---

1. A study commissioned by the National Commission on the Causes and Prevention of Violence, which was formed by President Johnson and which existed from 1968 to 1969. The study was named for study director Daniel Walker, who later became governor of Illinois. The Walker Report declared that the police were to blame for the violence in Chicago and referred to the event as a "police riot."

A well-dressed woman saw this incident and spoke angrily to a nearby police captain. As she spoke, another policeman came up from behind her and sprayed something in her face with an aerosol can. He then clubbed her to the ground. He and two other policemen then dragged her along the ground to the same paddy wagon and threw her in.

Meanwhile Dellinger and the group he was with had finally made it to the street in front of the Hilton. He remembers the scene as follows:

As I approached, several vans came up a side street and unloaded police reinforcements. The new arrivals jumped out of the vans and charged into the crowd, swinging their clubs and chanting, "Kill, kill, kill."

We had no sound system capable of reaching the crowd, no plan of action, no training of marshals (most of whom were scattered, arrested, or bleeding from previous assaults) adequate for the occasion. All day long I had felt betrayed by the absence of most of the movement's pacifist leadership, some of whom had stayed away from Chicago altogether, some of whom had engaged in a small, separatist "pacifist action" the day before, aloof from the major dynamics of the week's struggle. Meanwhile a number of the more vocal, visible leaders had been arguing for several hours that "This is the end of nonviolence in America. It simply won't work anymore." I felt completely defeated by the situation, incapable of doing anything useful.

I shall never forget the spontaneous actions of the demonstrators. Of course, some rocks flew and some fists went into action in attempts to ward off the attackers—desperate acts of angry self-defense. But mainly the protestors parried the blows while retreating slowly and in remarkably good order, then surged forward again as each police attack momentarily spent itself. . . . It took a long time to push us back, to clear the streets for a couple of blocks. And when the streets were finally cleared and lined with police, the demonstrators were still there, massed on the grass across from the hotels, chanting antiwar slogans, singing movement songs, shouting to the delegates.

Another Rally the Next Day

Meanwhile, back at the convention, Humphrey had been nominated, McCarthy defeated, and a number of the delegates had returned to their hotels, only to become swept up in the melee around the Hilton.

Mayor Daley would later complain that his administration and the Chicago police did not get sympathetic press and TV coverage from their actions of Wednesday night.

On Thursday, August 29, a crowd of some 5,000 gathered in the strip of park opposite the Hilton for another rally sponsored by National Mobe. According to the original schedule this was to have been a "massive People's Assembly to project the directions and tasks" which were supposed to have developed out of the workshops and activities of the week. But McCarthy turned out to be the principal speaker.

Formally, the National Mobe rally was adjourned before McCarthy was introduced, but neither the major media nor the bulk of the crowd drew the fine distinction. The crowd gave McCarthy a standing ovation, and he emerged as the martyr of the hour.

After McCarthy spoke, another attempt was made to march to the Amphitheatre. This time some 2,000 people led by [African American comedian] Dick Gregory and [political activist] Eric Weinberger, as well as a number of accredited delegates to the convention, made it as far as Michigan Avenue and Eighteenth Street where they were stopped by police and National Guard units. Only delegates would be allowed beyond this point, they were told.

About twenty-five of the delegates, including columnist Murray Kempton, removed their badges, moved forward with Gregory and some fifty others, and submitted to arrest. Then police and guardsmen tear-gassed the rest of the crowd and chased it north, back toward the Hilton and Grant Park, where sporadic demonstrating and attacks by the police and National Guard continued until early morning.

About 5:00 A.M. Friday, police raided a suite on an upper floor of the Hilton rented by John Kenneth Galbraith and others and used as a McCarthy headquarters. (The cops claimed that ever since Wednesday night people in the hotel had been throwing ashtrays, beer cans, and other things out the windows at them, and that they had pinpointed this suite as a source of such missiles.) The last of the demonstrators were leaving the street by 8:30 in the morning. The Chicago Democratic Party demonstrations were over.

Some 660 people had been arrested in connection with the actions, probably over 1,000 injured, and one killed. He was Dean Johnson, a seventeen-year-old Native American from South Dakota who was in Old Town when the police made a sweep. He allegedly drew a gun on them and was shot down.

Remembering the Kent State Massacre

Lilian Tyrrell

On April 30, 1970, President Nixon stunned Americans when he announced that U.S. and South Vietnamese troops would move from Vietnam into neighboring Cambodia. This announcement galvanized protesters around the nation, particularly at colleges and universities. Kent State University in Ohio was no different: On Friday, May 1, 1970, students there organized a rally protesting the invasion of Cambodia and burned a copy of the U.S. constitution. The protesters agreed to meet again for a protest on May 4, then left the rally, with some breaking windows in the town and clashing with police that evening. After viewing the damage and hearing rumors of a radical plot, the Kent city mayor declared a state of emergency, and the governor of Ohio agreed to send assistance. The following day, over one thousand protesters surrounded the headquarters of the campus Reserve Officer Training Corps (ROTC) and managed to burn down the building. Firefighters were forced to give up efforts to save the building after their hoses were slashed by onlookers. Following these events units of the Ohio State National Guard moved onto campus, clearing the scene and forcing students and nonstudents alike into dormitories, where many spent the night.

The next morning the campus, which was entirely occupied by the National Guardsmen was strangely calm, but by evening there had been another confrontation between protesters and police and National Guardsmen. On May 4, after two thousand people gathered on campus in defiance of orders banning the rally, the National Guard used tear gas and bayonets to force the crowd to disperse. When the crowd remained, twenty-eight of the Guardsmen turned and fired at the gathered protesters. Four Kent State students (William Knox Schroeder, Sandra Lee Scheuer, Jeffrey Glen Miller, and Allison Krause) were killed by the gunfire, and nine others (also Kent State students) were wounded, some seriously. The "Kent State Massacre" shocked the nation and inspired strikes and protests at hundreds of colleges and universities around the country.

Shortly before the Kent State Massacre, Lilian Tyrrell moved from England to Ohio with her husband after he was hired as a professor at the university. In this article, which is an excerpt from an interview she gave to the Kent State Oral History Project in 1995, Tyrrell describes what it was like being on campus during the protests and the massacre. Tyrrell, who has also taught at Kent State University, is an internationally recognized fiber artist who creates tapestries describing contemporary events.

The Thursday, it must have been April the 31st [sic], I believe —there was a rally and anti-war demonstration held on the Commons and I'd heard about it on WKSU [the Kent State University radio station] and also I think maybe it was in—advertised in the student paper, but I definitely heard about it more than once. And, I thought, "Oh, God, there'll be a crowd down there." And I went down, and I took my son because my daughter was in Kindergarten, my son was only 3½, so I took him with me. And we went to the Commons and I didn't even think I was in the right place to begin with because there was so few people, there was about somewhere between 30, maybe 50 people at the maximum. And a lot of those people, once I had sat down on the grass, seemed to be keeping an eye on us more than actually part of the students who were demonstrating. A lot of officious-looking people, or official-looking people maybe I should say, they were sort of walking around. Some of them, I think one or two of them had cameras. And it was really quite pathetic, because they didn't seem to be very experienced—the speakers—they all stood up and starting saying their usual sort of rhetoric. . . . And I sat down on the grass with my son and he played around and made sort of noises to the people around me and everyone seemed to be just enjoying the sunshine, basically.

Friday evening, the bars closed, but, I—when the bikers came into town, they closed the bars and I only heard stories about that I wasn't there—from students how they had been pushed out of the bars, how they had to leave their drinks and their food, and how they'd been pushed out onto the street and verbally abused and then a few of them lit fires—sort of little fires in the middle of the road, and tempers rose and people got agitated—but that was—I wasn't there, so basically I can only rely on what people told me who were there.

The Burning of the ROTC Building

The next night, Saturday night, was when the ROTC [Reserve Officer Training Corps] Building closed. I was—I was at a Dick Myers film festival, downtown, in one of the buildings that was close to the ROTC Building. And we were sort of just watching the films, and we were ready to go home—or a little before we were ready to go home—I think it was Craig Lucas, came up and said, "We're locked in the building, we can't get out." And I said, "What do you mean?" And he said, "We can't get out of the building, the National Guard is on campus and we can't get out of the building." And I said, "Well, that's ridiculous, I'm going home! I've got a babysitter. She told me she had to be home by eleven o'clock. I have got to go home, I've got two children to look after!" And sure enough, we went downstairs, they would not let us out and I'm saying—and I'm screaming at the Guardsmen—I'm saying, "But, you can't keep me in here, I've got to go home to my children!" And they said, "Nobody is leaving this building." And we went back into the building, and we searched all over the building for a telephone that worked. Well, for some reason, not one of the telephones that we found worked. I couldn't phone up my babysitter. We were kept in there—oh, at least two hours, two and a half hours, I can't remember exactly how long at this point. But, I was terrified because I was—and everyone was saying, "Don't worry, you know, Jo [Joan?] is a good babysitter, she won't leave the children." And I kept saying, "But she told me she had to, her father is very strict. She absolutely had to be home by this point in time." And I was really angry that these people had locked me into the building and I couldn't get home to my children. And then, finally they let us out—we had realized that the ROTC Building had been closed and regardless. . . .

(Interviewer, interrupting) Was burning at that point.

Was it still burning? Well—it, by that time it was—1:00. Things had calmed down. And we walked—we didn't go right that way, but we walked close enough that we could see some of the damage and stuff. But, the [Ohio State National] Guardsmen were a little freaky, a little nervous. And we went home.

Not much happened on the Sunday that I can remember. And it seemed that everything had come back to normal. Now, I had heard that there was going to be a protest on—well, maybe I should talk about Sunday, too because various times during this period of time, over the four days when the Guards were there I had gone onto campus to meet my husband often [?] taking the children. And I remember that the Guardsmen and their attitude gradually deteriorated over those four days to such a point where they were blatantly antagonistic. And, my daughter who was five at the time would like skip ahead of the push-chair. And you'd look up and you'd see Guardsmen with their rifles trained on her head following her down the road with their rifles trained on her. And you'd turn around and look at them and they would laugh in your face as if to say, you know, "We have the power here." And, it was really amazing that they felt free—if they were trained soldiers, why were they behaving in this way? Why were they trying to intimidate us? And I think everybody who was connected with the University felt that antagonism—felt they were being pushed around and threatened and—well began to be building up [?] a head of steam that we're not going to be pushed around, I don't think you can treat people in that way without—especially not educated people who are used to freedom—treat them in that way and expect not to have a reaction.

Going to the Demonstration

So, on the Monday I wanted to go to the demonstration, but I knew there was a lot of people going to be going there. And I also knew the Guard were on campus and because of the atmosphere I wasn't sure I should because I had to look after my son and I would have had to have taken him with me. And in the end [?], I felt angry enough that I was going to go anyway. So, I walked up to the campus with my son. And I wasn't—I didn't actually see the shootings. I was with a group of students who were on the other side of the hill, sort of halfway up, on the level sort of with the Victory Bell, but closer to the Art Building. And I was standing with a group of people there and you could feel the atmosphere getting very tense. And, I was talking to some guys who were standing beside me and they were sort of talking about the Guardsmen and I was basically not saying anything, I was just listening to what was happening. And then it—I heard what sounded like firecrackers and the guy turned to me and he said, "I'm a Vietnam veteran, and that's REAL gunfire, get the hell out of here!" And I said, "Oh, yes, OK." But my first reaction was to hold tight onto the rail because I didn't want to be pushed around. I didn't want to run away. But, I did have my son with me, who was 3½, and I—I know I've got to get him out of here. If it was me—just me—I think I probably would have stayed because I felt so angry. But, as it was, I just ran with the rest of the crowd, got out of there, got a bus home. And everybody on the campus bus going—I was going up to the Main Street—everybody was—was silent in the bus. I think most of the people had come from the Commons and had knew [sic] what had happened. It was—and every so often, somebody at the back was swearing and saying, you know, "F—," and things like that "F— them, F— them," you know. So, it was a very strange bus ride. I think the anger that you felt and the frustration. . . . And I just got off and started walking up to my street. At which point, one of my neighbors came flying towards me, screaming. And I didn't know what had happened. And as she came by, I grabbed her and I said, "Barbie [or Bobby?], what's wrong?" And she said, "I've got to get to the school, they're killing the Guardsmen!" And I—at that point, I didn't know who had died—and I just, 'cause I could only have one hand—I just dug my hand into her and I said, "Do be reasonable, stop and think about this for a minute. I don't think any Guardsmen are killed. If anyone's killed, it's like students." And I said, you know, "Calm down, no one's going to hurt your children." "I've got to get up to the school to save my children from the students!" And I was saying, "This is ridiculous, you know, the students have children of their own in those schools, no one's going to hurt the children." I couldn't believe this woman had freaked out to that extent. Finally she calmed down and then she started walking, but she was still going to the school. She still was going to save her children. By the time I got home, which was like a few houses down, got into my house.

Children Were Traumatized

A little while afterwards, my daughter came home from Kindergarten. And she rushed into the door, and she was totally traumatized. She said, "Mommy, is there a war?" And I said, "No, darling, there is not a war, come and talk to me about it." And she said, "Suddenly, we were all rushed into the buses and made to lie on the floor of the buses so that no one would hurt us. And the soldiers were shouting all the time, screaming at us to 'Stay down, stay down!'" And they drove the children home. And the children were traumatized, they—I mean, she was traumatized. She thought there was a war on, she thought someone was going to kill us. And, so I calmed her down and I talked to her. By the next morning—I don't think there was any school the next day for the children, because I remember it must have been a Tuesday morning, but she wanted to go out and play with her friends. It was the children of the same woman I had stopped running down the road. And they had—any day they were at home they went to play with their friends in their sandbox. And she wanted to go and play with them. And William wanted to go and play with them. And I said,

"Well, OK"—'cause it was only like two houses down, all they to do was walk across a little bit of grass to get there—and I said, "OK, but that's the only place you're allowed to go and I want you to come straight back home afterwards." And they went out. And it was about ten—well, about fifteen minutes later, ten minutes later, they came charging back for the door again, my daughter was hysterical and she's holding her brother for dear life and screaming and his face was just covered in blood. And she said, "They threw stones at us, Mommy, and I came home!" That all the children in the sandbox that were usually their friends had—I don't know what their parents had said to them, that they thought they could go out and do this—but they'd all collected stones and they threw stones at them when they came. And, well I, I—at that point, I felt, OK, this is a really freaky situation—I'm—you can't trust anybody, these people are [untelligible], they're sort of crazy. And I decided they weren't going anywhere without me. And everywhere they went, even if it was just out into our little piece of garden, I went with them or I watched them from the window. And, the children were really traumatized. And, like I was in Hahn's one day, it must have been a week or two after the shootings and I had turned around to get some things off the shelf to buy, you remember the Hahn's coffee shop in town on Main—on, um,

(Interviewer, interrupting) Water . . .

Water Street, right, then I turned around and I saw my daughter's face, she was sort of cowering and terrified. And there was a big policeman sort of jumping up and down in front of her, you know, I think he was trying to actually be nice to her and—but, it was so frightening because she was so terrified and I remember just leaving whatever I was doing and throwing myself in front of him and screamed at him, "Leave my daughter alone! Don't you get near her! Get away from her!" I guess he professed [?] that I was a mad woman or something, I don't think he was meaning to terrify her, but she was totally terrified. And I reacted like that because I think we were all a little reactional. And I think over that long summer, I think we were all—it was a really horrible summer.

CHAPTER 3

Soldiers and Veterans

Vietnam Letters

Letters from Soldiers and Dependents

Those who served in the military during the Vietnam War comprised almost 10 percent of their generation.

During the Vietnam era (between 1964 and 1975) over 9 million military personnel served on active duty, of whom 2.6 million served in the countries surrounding Vietnam or in Vietnam itself. Over fifty-eight thousand Americans died during the conflict, with another three hundred thousand wounded. Some of the most poignant and telling sources from the Vietnam era are the letters that those serving in the military sent to their friends and loved ones and the letters that they received in return.

The first letter in this excerpt was sent to Specialist 4th Class Kenneth Peeples Jr., who had arrived in Vietnam in June 1966, by his parents. Peeples was wounded in action in February 1967 and was recovering in a hospital when he received this letter. After recovering and returning home, Peeples went back to college and eventually earned master's degrees in library science and education. He later became the head of the reference department at LaGuardia Community College Library in the City University of New York.

The second letter in this excerpt was written by Brian Sullivan, a lieutenant assigned to the 1st Marine Division, and was sent to his then-wife Tobie. Sullivan was a field artillery officer and infantry platoon commander in the area around Da Nang from June 1968 to June 1969 and, as he recounts in this letter, was used to losing soldiers in the fierce fighting in that area. After the war Sullivan taught history at Yale University, became a Senior Fellow at the National Defense University, and worked with the U.S. Air Force Space Command.

Bernard Edelman, ed., *Dear America: Letters Home from Vietnam*. New York: W.W. Norton & Company, 1985. Copyright © 1985 by The New York Vietnam Veterans Memorial Commission. All rights reserved. Reproduced by permission of the editor.

The third letter in this excerpt is a letter from Eleanor Wimbish to her son, William R. (Billy) Stocks, who served with the 23rd Infantry Division and who died in 1969. This letter, written in 1984, was left under Stocks's name on the Vietnam Veterans Memorial in Washington, D.C. Wimbish has left a series of such letters at the Wall; her letters have appeared in numerous books, news articles, and television specials on the Vietnam conflict.

From Parents to a Wounded Son

February 21, 1967
St. Eleutherus
7:30 P.M.

Hello Son,

How are you feeling today? Hope this letter will find you successfully recovering. Today we received your Purple Heart medal [which you received for being wounded]. I looked at it with mixed emotions. Happy, because you are out of Vietnam; sad, because of the price you had to pay to get away from there. However, I do hope that you won't have any serious complications and that you will fully recover and be restored to health. I also realize the thousands of boys who will never return home, and the parents who have received the Purple Heart because of their son's death. When I think of these things, I know that I shouldn't feel too bad about your condition. Our main concern now is your recovery!

Let me say here and now that I'm extremely proud of you, son. Not because you were awarded the Heart, but because you did an honorable thing. I know that you were bitterly against going into the service and rejected our reasons for being in Vietnam. I also knew of your feelings about the U.S. and its treatment of Negroes. I also imagine that you were contemplating going AWOL. Yet, in spite of these conditions, you did everything that was asked of you. Whether it was to please your mother or your grandmother I do not know.

But I do know that you made a prudent and honorable decision. It may not matter at all to you, but you are coming home a hero to us. Not a war hero, because you had to fight and get shot, but more so because you made a man's decision and stuck it out. You should feel proud of yourself! You are now in a position to take every advantage that is offered to a GI (and there are many). You can hold your head high everywhere you go, and you can go anywhere you wish. Had you chosen the alternative, these things would not be so. I hope Richard will realize these things and take that "chip" off of his shoulders!

Everyone here is so concerned about you, all of our friends constantly ask about you. Your mother told one person about you on the telephone, and a few days later the whole parish knew. Certainly will be glad when you are sent stateside. Let us know as soon as you find out. . . .

You know, I was thinking that for a person who never traveled much, you are really seeing the world. Who would have thought that you would be writing from Japan, and your letters would arrive here in just two days. Hope ours reach you just as fast.

Rest good, and eat hearty. Relax, and don't worry about anything. Will write again soon. Until then, may God continue to bless you.

Love,
Mom & Pop

A Platoon Commander to His Wife

March 2 [1969]

Darling,

I love you so very, very much. Finally it's over for a while and I can write. I don't know where to begin or what to say or how. I guess I'll just try to tell you how I feel, which is mostly proud, sad, tired and relieved. After all these endless days and nights, they gave me and the platoon 36 hours off. I spent today going to memorial services for my people, doing wash, catching up on work in my office and writing up people for medals.

Oh, Darling, it's been so unreal. I'm not going to go into detail—it would only scare, depress or worry you. Just be convinced I'm fine, it's over and all I have to complain of now is a bad cold and a lot of fatigue. These last days were just so filled with fighting, marching, thinking, all the time thinking, "Am I doing it right? Is this what they said at Quantico? How can I be sure I haven't led us into a trap and the [North Vietnamese Army] NVA are waiting?" etc., etc., until I became so exhausted just by worrying. I'm just so grateful (to whom?). I "only" lost six men (I *know* how awful that sounds)! I had a seventh guy fall off a cliff and get a bad cut and concussion, but he'll be OK.

I'm so confused. At the services today they were talking about God protecting people and eternal life and I felt so desolate, so despairing. I know there is no reward waiting for them or any hope. I began crying I felt so awful and hopeless, but somehow held it back and it just looked like I was sniffling from my cold. (See! How awful my ego and pride that I couldn't even let myself weep for those poor, poor kids!) All I can say is that considering how awful it was, I'm so lucky I didn't lose more.

I said I was proud. Mostly of them. I'm putting 10 of them in for decorations. Enclosed are some of the rough drafts of citations. Don't read them if you don't want to. Just save them for me. I guess I should be honest. I've been nominated, I hear, for the Silver Star, the third highest medal. Please don't get upset. I didn't try to win it—I was just trying to keep my people alive and doing the best I could. I may not even get it, 'cause the reviewing board might knock it down to a Bronze Star. You know me so well, you know I'm lying if I say I'm not pleased. I am, I'm proud, but only the worst part of me. My better part is just so sad and unhappy this whole business started.

Again, though it may be foolish, I'll keep my word and be honest. The post-Tet offensive isn't over. All intelligence points to a return bout. However, my platoon is 1,000% better than it was, we have so much support now—like a family, really. We'll all watch out for each other. Also, we don't believe they'll hit again near here, so whatever happens, I'll be OK. That's the truth too, honey. I have fantastic good luck, as strange as that may sound, and what's US is too good and too strong for any badness.

Love,
Brian

To a Dead Son, Left at the Wall

Dear Bill,

Today is February 13, 1984. I came to this black wall again to see and touch your name, and as I do I wonder if anyone ever stops to realize that next to your name, on this black wall, is your mother's heart. A heart broken 15 years ago today, when you lost your life in Vietnam.

And as I look at your name, William R. Stocks, I think of how many, many times I used to wonder how scared and homesick you must have been in that strange country called Vietnam. And if and how it might have changed you, for you were the most happy-go-lucky kid in the world, hardly ever sad or unhappy. And until the day I die, I will see you as you laughed at me, even when I was very mad at you, and the next thing I knew, we were laughing together.

But on this past New Year's Day, I had my answer. I talked by phone to a friend of yours from Michigan, who spent your last Christmas and the last four months of your life with you. Jim told me how you died, for he was there and saw the helicopter crash. He told me how you had flown your quota and had not been scheduled to fly that day. How the regular pilot was unable to fly, and had been replaced by someone with less experience. How they did not know the exact cause of the crash. How it was either hit by enemy fire, or they hit a pole or something unknown. How the blades went through the chopper and hit you. How you lived about a half hour, but were unconscious and therefore did not suffer.

He said how your jobs were like sitting ducks. They would send you men out to draw the enemy into the open and *then* they would send in the big guns and planes to take over. Meantime, death came to so many of you.

He told me how, after a while over there, instead of a yellow streak, the men got a mean streak down their backs. Each day the streak got bigger and the men became meaner. Everyone but *you*, Bill. He said how you stayed the same, happy-go-lucky guy that you were when you arrived in Vietnam. How your warmth and friendliness drew the guys to you. How your [lieutenant] gave you the nickname of "Spanky," and soon your group, Jim included, were all known as "Spanky's gang." How when you died it made it so much harder on them for you were their moral support. And he said how you of all people should never have been the one to die.

Oh, God, how it hurts to write this. But I must face it and then put it to rest. I know that after Jim talked to me, he must have relived it all over again and suffered so. Before I hung up the phone I told Jim I loved him. Loved him for just being your close friend, and for sharing the last days of your life with you, and for being there with you when you died. How lucky you were to have him for a friend, and how lucky he was to have had you.

Later that same day I received a phone call from a mother in Billings, Montana. She had lost her daughter, her only child, a year ago. She needed someone to talk to for no one would let her talk about the tragedy. She said she had seen me on [television] on New Year's Eve, after the Christmas letter I wrote to you and left at this memorial had drawn newspaper and television attention. She said she had been thinking about me all day, and just had to talk to me. She talked to me of her pain, and seemingly needed me to help her with it. I cried with this heartbroken mother, and after I hung up the phone, I laid my head down and cried as hard for her. Here was a mother calling me for help with her pain over the loss of her child, a grown daughter. And as I sobbed I thought, how can I help her with her pain when I have never completely been able to cope with my own?

They tell me the letters I write to you and leave here at this memorial are waking others up to the fact that there is still much pain left, after all these years, from the Vietnam War.

But this I know. I would rather to have had you for 21 years, and all the pain that goes with losing you, than never to have had you at all.

Mom

Black and in the Army

Stanley Goff, with Clark Smith

Approximately 250,000 African American officers and men served in Vietnam itself as anything from infantrymen to supply clerks to fighter pilots during the war; many more served in the military in other parts of the world during the same period. Stanley Goff was one of those African Americans who found themselves drafted and then sent to Vietnam. In this excerpt from *Brothers: Black Soldiers in the Nam*, Goff describes his experience as a young African American drafted into the U.S. Army. In many ways Goff's experiences matched those of other soldiers (of all races, ethnicities, and colors) who served in Vietnam: He found a close buddy during training, endured the weeks of basic training that are pictured in every movie about the army, and discovered things that he both liked and hated about the military. Like many—though by no means all—of the draftees and recruits, Goff was not particularly against the war. Upon finishing his training he felt as though he was prepared for combat in Vietnam. "We were ready to go to Vietnam," he recalls. "At first, yeah, I was concerned. I was scared. Then I wasn't."

While in many ways Goff's experiences were like those of any other soldier, Goff's identity as an African American affected how he viewed the military and how he was treated as a soldier. The army, he found—or at least parts of it—was largely inhabited by other African Americans, though some parts of the military remained almost segregated. Many of Goff's fellows in Advanced Infantry Training (AIT) were African American, as were most of the sergeants with combat experience, who were teaching the advanced students. The overwhelming majority of the officers and the other soldiers were Caucasian, however, and as a result African American troops were sometimes discriminated against. As Goff points out in other sections of his book, racial tensions were running high throughout the entire Vietnam period, and those tensions certainly affected those serving in the military. This excerpt provides a clear description of what entering the U.S. Army was like for hundreds of thousands of African Americans who were swept up by the draft and sent off to Vietnam.

Arriving at the induction center in Oakland was very, very depressing. I took the bus over from San Francisco. There was the huge grayish building with glass all the way around that I'd been avoiding for months and months. You couldn't see inside. It looked bleak, and I cursed. It looked bleak because I was bleak. A few guys were standing around outside, but inside there was this huge sea of guys. They were sitting on benches like church pews, just like a congregation for young men only. It felt strange; here I was getting ready to be carted off. I was a black and I thought about slavery. You know, the guys were predominantly black. It's right there. You don't have to be academically accomplished to ask, "Aren't there any other races to be drafted aside from blacks?" At least 70 percent of the guys in my group were black, and I'm being very conservative.

In the room there was a general hum and murmur of people being processed. There was a big desk about twenty-five feet square. Names were called, forms filled out. It's called processing. I did a lot of processing in the armed forces. I did nothing but process all the damn time.

Meeting a Buddy

I saw Bob the first time inside of the induction center waiting to be processed. When I went to the front desk, he was sitting there staring at me. I was staring around at the mass of faces, and all of a sudden, our eyes locked. His eyes were very cold and depressed. I could almost see the hurt and anguish he was going through just sitting there. Maybe that was what caught my eye. I had no responsibilities myself. I wasn't married. I didn't want to be there, but what the heck. I had just come out to the Gold City of San Francisco and I wasn't having that many breaks. My mother was here but living in poverty. I saw that he had a "Why me?" feeling, and I guess I felt the same way.

Bob was sturdy, well-built, a very alert black; intelligence just written on his face. He seemed like a guy who would be very fluent with the ladies. I used to love to play around myself. When you run with another guy that you know has no problems about women, you can have a hell of a lot of fun. He sort of reminded me of myself. He probably thought the same thing.

When I saw him again five or six hours later getting ready to go out of the building, we looked at each other; no smile or anything. He was shaking his head and we both said at the same time, "What the shit are we doing here, man?" We'd been inducted; we were in the armed forces. It felt so cold and lifeless. It was like we were programmed to die, just going out there to die, that's all.

Anyway, we left the building and went on over to the USO. We were both a little reserved because I guess he didn't want me to think that he was harping on me, and I didn't want him to think that I was harping on him. Even though I liked him, I didn't want it to be obvious. It's sort of strange what men go through. I guess we were both wary of a leech-type of guy. I wanted to check him out from a distance. We were talking small talk across the room. We met another brother whose name was Jamie and were kidding him about his real nice Afro that he had: "He's gonna have to get rid of that Afro, no doubt about it," "Yeah!," "No kidding," "Right on."

Beginning Training at Fort Lewis, Washington

Our orders were all the same. We were all going to Fort Lewis, Washington. I'd never been anywhere but Texas and San Francisco; here I was going to Fort Lewis, Washington. Where the hell was that? Was that the state of Washington, or was that

Washington, DC? I didn't know. Somebody said Tacoma. Shit, where was that?

We flew right to this Air Force base near Tacoma and were bused out to Fort Lewis where we were met by a little turd of a corporal, a little skinny guy with a crooked nose.

He waited till we got off the bus, and then he started hollering, "OK, God damn it, get out, you're in the Army now, stop slopping around, get your God damn ass over here." He was real young; had a couple of stripes on him. He herded us around in front of the barracks; told us "OK, God damn it, you gonna get all this long hair cut. You're in the Army now and all the bullshit stops." It was sort of a psychological induction. Getting ready to go gung ho.

A bunch of guys were milling around inside the barracks. Smoke was happening all over, and guys were finding out where other guys were from. Bob and Jamie and I were looking around at the white guys and we're talking about them: "Oh, man, look at these God damn guys; I wonder where they're from?" The whole group was about 65 percent black, and we're wondering how this was going to work out. Bob and I hadn't been around a lot of white guys. Jamie had been, to a certain degree. He was jumping right into it with those guys. We started hearing guys from the South, you know, from Alabama and Georgia. . . .

A Black Sergeant

We were really straight, square guys. But we did a lot of growing up in the armed forces. We were really pretty innocent about everything—government, society. We didn't want to make any trouble. We went out there and did what this guy said to do and tried to make the best of it.

Bob and I ended up in the same platoon with a black platoon sergeant. We felt indifferent to this, but at least he was black. We knew and know now that all the drill sergeants were bastards. They were the roughest men we'd ever met throughout our entire stay in the army. They were nasty. I mean really nasty. But it was due to that intense training that we even got through the Nam. Seriously!

There were about forty guys in our platoon, about fifteen blacks, fifteen whites, and ten other minorities. Drill Sergeant Payne ran the 3d platoon—a Nam drill sergeant. I looked him over. He was a flamboyant type with a thick moustache, tan skin, lanky. Even though he was hollering and saying the same bullshit as the other sergeants, I got a different feeling about him; maybe because he was black. I don't know. Maybe this guy was okay—maybe he was just following the rules and wasn't a bad guy.

Drill Sergeant Payne was with us for a while, and then all of a sudden he was gone, disappeared, or transferred, and we had no drill sergeant. That was beautiful. Drill Sergeant Tadlock used to come over and put his foot in our ass. Then he'd go back and put his foot in his own platoon's ass. The other drill instructors used to say we were motherless. Tadlock was a very slim, very solid, middle-aged guy. He was about forty years old and fit as a taut fiddle. I really admired the guy as a great specimen of a man. I mean on the inside too. He could convey his inner spirit to us. We found that he was damned serious and very concerned about the men. We could read it in him. Even though he was very, very mean, we could tell that he was sincere. He felt that it was his responsibility whether we made it through the Nam or not. He felt that if he didn't teach us right, we were going to go over there and get mutilated. That was his thing. It wasn't us personally. He didn't care whether our name was John or Dick.

Rigorous Training

We would go out on long runs, all day long with a full pack. We ran to the mess hall. We never did walk on that fort at all. The only time we got a chance to walk was on Sundays. At night I would be hurting so bad I couldn't even go to sleep. I felt I was maybe dying, my body was undergoing such a tremendous change.

Doing all those push-ups was really something. I would think that I couldn't do but five or ten push-ups. Fifty push-ups? Nobody could do fifty push-ups! And all of a sudden I was doing eighty-five; no problem.

In the beginning of basic I couldn't run a square block without falling out. At the end I was doing the mile in six minutes flat. Six minutes flat, me? That was unheard of. You know, not me, man. And I was doing it. That was what the drill sergeants made possible.

Bob and I were constantly feeding each other encouragement to perform and not drop out. There were times when Bob wanted to give up—just quit and go AWOL. His old lady was pregnant and since they weren't married, the army didn't give him an allotment. He was only making ninety-one dollars a month and he worried about that. We knew that as draftees we'd be going to the Nam. That was no secret, but I told Bob that if we made it back, we'd be okay and running off would only be trouble. He could get married when he went home on leave so when the baby came the maternity thing would be taken care of by the government. So I talked him out of going AWOL. We really stuck tight. He was counting on going home after AIT (Advanced Individual Training) and taking care of everything.

Besides physical training, Tadlock would have us go out on the range for bayonet practice. The guy showed us how one wrong move and we'd be dead. We learned hand-to-hand combat, how to kill a man fast, how to break down a weapon and put it back together. We learned how to fire the M-16 rifle and the M-60 machine gun.

I remember one incident on the firing range. I didn't have the weapon held right while I was firing. Drill Sergeant Meckler came along and kicked me hard right in the side. He was a racist bastard and I really felt like shooting him down. All I had to do was just turn right around. That was what my mind started telling me. And then I started realizing that I wasn't playing any more. This was a serious thing that I was into. This was reality. A man comes up who had the authority to just kick me in the God damn ribs because he was who he was. All I had to do was just roll over, and pull the trigger, and just blow this motherf—— apart. I never felt that way toward anybody before then. But I just pretended like he was out there at that target, and I blew him away that way, because I knew if I didn't do it that way, all was lost with my life.

Learning from the Instructors

Out on the weapon training areas the atmosphere was different. The sergeants out on the range weren't hard like the drill instructors. Most of them were into really teaching what they were supposed to teach. We never heard any guy that had an attitude out on the range. I guess he wouldn't stay out there too long if he had.

The instructors were Vietnam combat veterans; they wore their Combat Infantry Badges. We would listen to these guys because they had been over there. The instructors told us about the units they had been in, what type of recognition the unit received. They'd say, "I saw a lot of guys get it." They might say something like that to alert us to the fact that we had better pay attention. "You can go to Vietnam and come back, if you remain alert. The strong can survive." They were telling us that most of the guys that got it were the guys that slipped up some way, made a mistake or figured that they were Superman. We could understand guys getting it in an ambush. That was nobody's fault; who knew who was hidden inside the brush? But I'm talking about guys that got killed when they took things for granted. A guy gets blown away by not taking enough caution. So basically, they were telling us about their experiences in the Nam and what we should do to better our chances.

The Indoctrination Takes Hold

The indoctrination finally took hold. We got to feel that these people knew what they were doing. Vietnam was always talked about as a joke. Nobody wanted to be in the gloom. Once we were into the war mentality, and once we were on the base, psychologically our training got to us. Even though we didn't want to succumb to it, we couldn't help it. When you do something over and over again, you have been programmed. I didn't know it then, but the Army knew it. And I know it now. We were brainwashed. You tell me brainwashing don't work? Bullshit. It worked. No doubt about it.

We were ready to go to Vietnam. Nobody was crying about it. Nobody was depressed about it, except some pussy guy, you know, some mother's baby. At first, yeah, I was concerned. I was scared. Then I wasn't. For people to be able to do this to you, you know that some brains are around there some place. And the instructors were very smart, too. They might not have had the best grammar in the world, but these guys knew what they were doing. I found this out, and I started getting confidence in what these guys were telling me. . . .

Finishing Basic Training

Basic ended on a Friday, and on Sunday we were going to another part of the fort. My orders were written up for AIT (Advanced Individual Training) at Fort Lewis. Bob's orders were also. That was where we lost Jamie. He went down to Fort Benning, I think it was.

The next day the drill sergeants hauled us out of the barracks, and Tadlock gave us his farewell speech: "We've trained you all. We know that we've given you the best training there is. You're going to go perhaps to another company that is not going to be as sharp and strict with discipline as we are. We know that basically wherever you go, you will be able to handle any type of circumstance. You should be able to, anyway. God damn it, I know damn well that I've put it into you. If you don't succeed, then it's your own God damn fault. And remember, there's only two kinds of guys in the Nam—the quick and the dead." And with that, the bus came. "Awright, God damn it, here's that bus, get your God damn ass outa here." That was it.

Tadlock was a very proud man. I never will forget how he stood there when we left him. His hands was on his hips and he was just staring at all of us, head never did move. I could tell he was just looking at all of us, and I guess he was just deciphering—who was going to make it back, who wasn't. Then he turned around and walked away.

We were ready for anything. Even though they said AIT was going to be a lot less hassle, we thought, bullshit. We were lined up in formation. Some guy came out of the CO's office, some kind of a special NCO that went to an NCO training school. They were losing so many sergeants in the war, they had to start this special NCO school, like Officer Candidate

School. These guys would come out of the NCO school like E-6s. So we had one that was going to be the company sergeant E-6; "acting first," they called him. I never will forget this son of a bitch. His name was Rocky. He was like an All-American, you know. The crewcut, blonde hair, blue-eyed kinda guy. They're hyper. He took over and started hollering. "All right, FALL OUT, N Company." We fell out, and he gave a big bull-shit speech about AIT. Then the regular drill sergeants finally all came out and we went back to our companies.

We got a black drill sergeant, Drill Sergeant Williams. Bob loved Drill Sergeant Williams. He was a very relaxed type of guy. It didn't seem like anything fazed him. He was an E-7, a combat veteran, a real pro. I think he said that he had been to Vietnam two times. He had earned his stripes the hard way—not like some of these "special" little buck sergeants. They couldn't tell him what to do, obviously. He had all this damn seniority, and like I said, he was a "field first" anyway. As company first, he was over Rocky, the acting company first. The rest of the drill sergeants were also black, which was very interesting.

Advanced Training Was Predominantly Black

Advanced Individual Training was predominantly black. That was why they had all those black drill sergeants, probably. Nothing but black guys in the whole f—ing company. That was particularly alarming to Bob and me. In fact, word was going around, and it wasn't a quiet word, that blacks were being drafted for genocidal purposes. Just to get rid of us—to eliminate the black male. And we believed it. There was a general consensus in 1968 that there must be a conspiracy against black youth. We didn't see any black officers coming out of training; we didn't see any black NCO trainees coming out. We saw lots of black drill sergeants, and they were all infantry, and they all had their Combat Infantry Badges. They had earned their stripes the hard way in Vietnam.

I think that those black drill sergeants had compassion for us, which is why they didn't just get right down on us, not su-perhard. I know a lot of times I felt proud for Williams. He was in for discipline, there was no doubt about that, as all the black drill sergeants were, but they didn't grind us in the dirt. I didn't know it then, but I know it now. They understood the racial imbalance; all these black young men that they knew were going to end on the front lines. They wanted to make sure that we got our training. Bullshit they didn't put up with. No doubt about that. . . .

Feeling Ready to Go to Vietnam

At that particular point in time, I started asking myself: "How do I feel about actually being ready to go? Can I protect myself when I go to Vietnam? Do I know enough? Do I have enough confidence in myself after AIT?" The answer was a resounding, yes. I felt that I was ready. I felt that I could protect myself. I knew what I was doing. Obviously, there was still a risk of getting wasted, but that was a chance that I would have to take. Hell, if I walked down the block I could be killed. Or, if I walked down to the club and got into it with another GI, I could be killed. I felt that I had all the tools that they equipped us with. If anybody stood a chance, I did. I was going to get back. I was psychologically ready to go. I'm not talking about the bureaucratic military government or me liking it. I'm talking about the confidence in what I had been taught. I'm talking about being prepared mentally for war; they had done it. I could only say, "Hell, they must know what they're doing." Undoubtedly I would not be of sound mind if I said they don't know what they're doing, and then said that I was ready to go over and die. I was ready to go over and survive.

Last Out of Saigon

Philip Caputo

After years of turmoil and protest, the United States pulled most of its personnel out of Vietnam in 1972 and 1973 as part of the "Vietnamization" of the war (turning over primary responsibility for the war to the South Vietnamese). A number of military advisers, intelligence operatives, diplomatic liaisons, and journalists did remain behind, however, and American attention continued to focus on the fate of South Vietnam. In 1975 the North Vietnamese Army (NVA) launched a massive offensive into the south; within days many powerful South Vietnamese military formations had collapsed, leaving the route clear for the North Vietnamese to seize the capital of Saigon and in effect end the war. North Vietnamese forces entered Saigon on April 30, 1975.

The last hours in Saigon were chaotic and terrifying. Those trying to leave before the North Vietnamese could take control included remaining Americans, visiting journalists, South Vietnamese women who had become involved with Americans or who had had children with American servicemen, and South Vietnamese who had worked with the Americans and whose opposition to communism guaranteed that they would be imprisoned and possibly executed by the North Vietnamese. Most of these would-be refugees were left behind. Images from the fall of Saigon were harrowing. Americans watched on their televisions as hundreds of South Vietnamese, in a scene even further popularized by the Broadway musical *Miss Saigon*, tried to scale the gates of the American embassy in Saigon in order to escape with the American helicopters, or as others

Philip Caputo, *A Rumor of War*. New York: Holt, Rinehart, and Winston, 1977, pp. 341–46. Copyright © 1977 by Philip Caputo. Reproduced by permission of Henry Holt and Company, LLC.

waited on the embassy rooftop helicopter pad for the final helicopters that never came. For many Americans, the fall of Saigon symbolized American defeat and humiliation.

In this except from *A Rumor of War*, which is a gripping memoir of a journalist's time in Vietnam, journalist and novelist Philip Caputo describes his own evacuation from Saigon on the day of its capture. Caputo had arrived at Da Nang in 1965 as a marine lieutenant with the first U.S. ground combat unit committed to fight in Vietnam. After leaving the military, Caputo joined the staff of the *Chicago Tribune* as a foreign correspondent and won a shared Pulitzer Prize in 1972 for reporting on election fraud in Chicago. Returning to Vietnam as a reporter, Caputo became one of the last Americans to leave Saigon in 1975. Philip Caputo is also the author of *Exiles: Three Short Novels* (1989) and *Means of Escape: A War Correspondent's Memoir of Life and Death in Afghanistan, the Middle East, and Vietnam* (2002).

An accurate description of the final month of North Vietnam's final campaign would require a book in itself. I am not even sure if what occurred could be called a campaign; a migration, rather. The North Vietnamese Army simply rolled over the countryside, driving on Saigon. Except for a brief, hopeless stand made by a single division at the provincial capital of Xuan Loc, the ARVN [Army of the Republic of Vietnam] offered no significant resistance. The South Vietnamese Army broke into pieces. It dissolved. There were terrible scenes of panicked soldiers beating and trampling civilians as they fled from the advancing enemy. Late in the month, the atmosphere of disintegration became palpable. Not just an army, but an entire country was crumbling, collapsing before our eyes. The roads were jammed with refugees and routed soldiers. Some of the columns were twenty miles long, winding out of the hills and rubber plantations toward the flat marshlands around Saigon. They stretched along the roads for as far as we could see, processions that seemed to have no beginning and no end. They shambled in the rain and heat: barefoot civilians;

soldiers whose boots were rotting on their feet, some still carrying their weapons and determined that their little bands would stick together, most without weapons, broken men determined only to escape; lost children crying for their parents, parents for their children; wounded men covered with dried blood and filthy battle dressings, some walking, some lying in heaps in the backs of ambulances; trucks, buses, herds of water buffalo, and oxcarts creaking on wooden wheels. They were packed densely and stretched down the roads, solid, moving masses that rolled over barricades and flowed past the hulks of burned-out tanks, past the corpses and pieces of corpses rotting in the fields at the roadsides. And from behind those retreating columns came the sound of bombs and shellfire, the guttural rumbling of the beast, war, devouring its victims.

There was so much human suffering in these scenes that I could not respond to it. It was numbing. Regardless of the outcome, I wanted to see it end. At the same time, a part of me did not want to see it end in a North Vietnamese victory. I kept thinking about Levy about Sullivan [two soldiers the authors had known], about all of the others, and something in me cried out against the waste of their lives. The war was lost, or very nearly lost. Those men had died for no reason. They given their all for nothing.

Personal Ambivalence About the War

I think these ambivalent feelings were typical of American veterans who, like me, were both opposed to the war and yet emotionally tied to it. After my discharge from the Marine Corps in mid-1967, I had drifted into the antiwar movement, though I was never passionately involved in it. I eventually joined the Vietnam Veterans Against the War, but my most explicit gesture of protest was made in 1970, when I mailed my campaign ribbons to President Nixon, together with a long and bitter letter explaining why I was opposed to American policies in Indochina. I thought, naïvely, that such a personal, individual act would have more effect than mass marches. About a month later, I received in the mail an envelope bearing the return address "The White House." It contained my medals and a curt note, written by some obscure functionary, which said that the Executive Branch of the United States government was not authorized to receive or hold military decorations; therefore, my ribbons were being returned to me. The writer concluded with the ominous phrase: "Your views about U.S. policies in South Vietnam have been noted and brought to the attention of the proper authorities." That episode sums up my career as an antiwar activist. My grand gesture of personal protest had been futile, as futile as the war itself. I seemed to have a penchant for lost causes.

Fleeing Saigon

[Fellow journalist Nicholas] Proffitt and I fell asleep in the early-morning hours. Lying on the floor behind the furniture with which I had barricaded the window, I was jarred awake when the North Vietnamese began shelling Tan Son Nhut Airport and part of the city with rockets and 130-mm field guns. It was April 29 [1975]. The bombardment went on for six hours. Around ten-thirty, a reporter who had a citizens' band radio tuned to the American embassy's frequency announced, "They've just passed the word. That's it. It's one-hundred-percent evacuation. It's bye-bye everybody."

A hasty, undignified exit followed. Crowds of newsmen, embassy officials, Vietnamese civilians, and various other "evacuees" stumbled down the half-deserted streets toward the evacuation points. I passed a group of ARVN militiamen and smiled at them wanly. "You go home now?" one of them asked. "Americans di-di?"

"Yes," I said, feeling like a deserter, "Americans di-di."

Moving to the Staging Area

Our motley column was eventually directed to a staging area across the street from a hospital. Columns of smoke were rising from the city's outskirts, and someone said that North Vietnamese troops had been spotted only two miles from where we were standing. We stood about, dripping sweat and listening to the steady thud of the incoming one-thirties. Finally, two olive-drab buses, led by a car with a flashing mars light, pulled up. We piled on board, some sixty or seventy crammed on each bus, the small convoy heading for Tan Son Nhut.

We were just passing through the airport's main gate as a South Vietnamese plane took off from the smoking, cratered runway. An old C-119 cargo plane, it had not climbed more than a few hundred feet when a spiraling fireball rose up behind it. There was a great boom as the anti-aircraft missile slammed into the C-119 and sent it crashing into the city. Our nervousness turned to fear, for we were to be evacuated by helicopter. Easy targets.

The buses stopped in front of a complex of buildings known as the Defense Attachés Office. During the height of American involvement in the war, the complex had been called Pentagon East. It had served as [General William] Westmoreland's headquarters. The tennis courts nearby were to be the landing zone for the helicopters. We clambered off the buses, spurred on by a heavy shell that banged into the tarmac seventy-five yards away. "Don't panic," someone said in a voice several octaves higher than normal.

Inside the building, we were lined up, divided into helicopter teams, and tagged. Every foot of every long corridor in the building was filled with Americans, Vietnamese refugees, newsmen from a dozen different countries, even a few old French plantation owners. The walls shook from the blasts of the shells hitting the runway. Small-arms fire crackled at the perimeter of the airbase. It was going to be a hot LZ [landing zone]. I hoped it would be my last one, and I tried not to think about those anti-aircraft missiles.

Catching the Helicopters

We sweated it out in there until the late afternoon, when the first of the Marine helicopters arrived. They were big CH-53s, each capable of holding as many people as a small airliner. "Okay, let's go!" yelled a Marine sergeant from the embassy guard. "Let's go. Drop all your luggage. No room for that. Move! Move! Move!" I dropped the valise I had lugged around all day and dashed out the door, running across the tennis courts toward the aircraft. Marine riflemen were crouched around the LZ, their weapons pointed toward the trees and rice paddies at the fringes of the airfield. Together with some sixty other people, half of them Vietnamese civilians and ARVN officers, I scrambled on board one of the CH-53s.

The helicopter lifted off, climbing rapidly. Within minutes, we were at six thousand feet, the wreckage of the South Vietnamese cargo plane burning far below. It was all so familiar: the deafening racket inside the helicopter; the door gunners crouched behind their machine guns, muzzles pointed down at the green and brown gridwork of the Mekong Delta through which flooded rivers spread like a network of blood vessels; and the expectant waiting—terrifying and yet exhilarating—as we looked for tracers or for the bright corkscrewing ball of a heat-seeking missile. One started to come up, but the lead helicopter in our flight diverted it with a decoy flare that simulated an aircraft engine's heat. We took some ground fire—fire from South Vietnamese soldiers who probably felt that the Americans had betrayed them.

My mind shot back a decade, to that day we had marched into Vietnam, swaggering, confident, and full of idealism. We had believed we were there for a high moral purpose. But somehow our idealism was lost, our morals corrupted, and the purpose forgotten.

"It Was Over"

We reached the coast about twenty minutes later. We were out of danger, out of range of the missiles, removed from all possibility of being among the last Americans to die in Vietnam. Relaxing their grip on the .50-caliber machine guns, the door gunners grinned and flashed the thumbs-up sign. Swooping out over the South China Sea, over the thousands of fishing junks jammed with refugees, the CH-53 touched down on the U.S.S. *Denver*, a helicopter assault ship that was part of the armada the Seventh Fleet had assembled for the evacuation. There was some applause as the aircraft settled down on the flight deck and as we filed out, a marine slapped me on the back and said, "Welcome home. Bet you're glad to be out of there." I was, of course. I asked him which outfit he was from.

"Ninth MEB," he answered. The 9th Expeditionary Brigade, the same unit with which I had landed at Danang. But the men who belonged to it now seemed a good deal more cynical than we who had belonged to it ten years before. The marine looked at the faint blue line marking the Vietnamese coast and said, "Well, that's one country we don't have to give billions of dollars to anymore."

The evacuees were processed and sent down to the scorching mess deck for a meal. Most of us were giddy with relief, but one disconsolate diplomat from the American Embassy just sat and muttered to himself, "It's over. It's the end. It's the end of an era. It was a lousy way to have it end, but I guess it had to end some way." Exhausted and sweating, he just shook his head. "The end of an era." I supposed it was, but I was much too tired to reflect on the historical significance of the event in which I had just taken part: America had lost its first war.

The next day, April 30, the ship's captain announced that the Saigon government had surrendered to the North Vietnamese. We took the news quietly. It was over.

A Professional Soldier's Perspective

Theodore L. Gatchel, interviewed by Carly Long

One of the problems those studying the Vietnam War or the Vietnam period face is the overwhelming abundance of antiwar books, documents, speeches, and letters. Students might well come to the conclusion after viewing this material that all but a few Americans were against the war and against involvement from the beginning. This conclusion, however, would be completely wrong; the members of the antiwar movements and the activists of the political Left were simply the *loudest* individuals in society during the 1960s. In fact, in the beginning the majority of Americans supported U.S. involvement in Vietnam. Only after the Tet Offensive in January 1968 did mainstream America really change its mind about the war. Many Americans who supported U.S. involvement did so quietly and without fanfare. The United States, they believed, was working to oppose the forces of communism and to maintain freedom around the world—both necessary tasks.

In this excerpt from a 1998 interview, Theodore L. Gatchel, who was a young Marine Corps officer in Vietnam, describes his feelings about the Vietnam War. Like many Americans, including both civilians and those in military service, Gatchel accepted the conflict in Vietnam as simply another necessary part of the Cold War and his participation in the conflict as part of his life in the military. "I didn't really even think so much in terms of whether I approved or disapproved of the war," he explains. "It was just a matter of what my job was." In the closing years of the war and afterward Gatchel's beliefs, if anything, became more firmly entrenched. "I don't think we were wrong to have been there, I think we went there with good intentions," he explains. "I think anybody that says that we were somehow morally wrong hasn't read much about communism."

Theodore L. Gatchel is a retired U.S. Marine Corps colonel and a professor of operations at the Naval War College in Newport, Rhode Island. After retiring from the military in 1991 he published several books and articles, including *At the Water's Edge: Defending Against the Modern Amphibious Assault* (Naval Institute Press, 1996), *Eagles and Alligators: An Examination of the Command Relationships That Have Existed Between Aircraft Carrier and Amphibious Forces During Amphibious Operations* (Naval War College Press, 1997), and a monthly newspaper column on military affairs for the *Providence Journal*. He was interviewed by Carly Long, who at the time was a student at South Kingston High School in Rhode Island.

Carly Long (CL): Do you recall how you felt as you left home, your family's reaction? What was your experience at boot camp or an officer training school?

Theodore Gatchel (TG): Well, when, you're talking about Vietnam, right? To leave for Vietnam? Well, when Vietnam came along, I'd already been an officer for almost five years so it was, and that was what, that was my job I mean it was just, if anything, I mean again, I was part of a unit that was called up to go to Vietnam as a unit in 1965. The only, my only reaction was that we had about less than a week to get our unit ready to go, go aboard ship and leave and get our families packed up, we were living on the West Coast at the time and so my wife had to get the house packed up and everything, and move, she was going to move back to the East Coast while I was gone. So, but it was, it was mainly just a professional concern, getting everything ready to go, so I'd be ready to go for what I figured would probably be a year and a very short period of time. . . .

Serving in Vietnam

CL: Okay. Where did you serve, if you went to Southeast Asia? When did you go? Where were you, and how long did you serve? How did you handle the news about the unpopularity of the war at home?

TG: Well, I served there twice. I went, the first time I went to Vietnam was 1965 and I went there with a US Marine Corps unit. And came back in the summer of 1966 and I went back again in 1969, served another year there with the Vietnamese Marines. So, I was there two separate times and I just really, once again, yeah we heard, we got the newspapers and heard on the radio about the protests that were going on. It just wasn't, you know, it really didn't really have much of an effect on, on what I was doing. I was busy enough, I wasn't concerned about what somebody was doing back at home who didn't like the war. It just didn't have much of an effect on me. Although there were some times that were kind of interesting as, on my first tour there I was a company commander, which meant that I was in command of a rifle company with about two hundred marines. And I had one of my marines bring in a flyer to me, and he was very worried it come from a girl that he knew in high school and she was in college and she had sent him this flyer that said something like, why are you out there fighting peasants who are only trying to protect their homes with pitch-forks and knives and what not. And this arrived just about the time that we started encountering North Vietnamese units that were armed with the best, the latest Soviet arms and weapons. In some ways they were better armed than we were. And this, I think this young marine thought he was going, he had some kind of subversive literature or something. He was worried about that. I told him to take it back, go and show it to your, I said well, have you shown it to any of your ship mates. He said yeah. I said what do they think. He said well, they thought it was a joke. I mean that was obviously pretty funny. I said well, go show it to the rest of them. Just show them what people back there, what, you know what they think about the war and what, and how misinformed they are as to, if they think we're out here fighting peasants that are armed with pitchforks and knives. But, you know basically, we had a job to do out there and we weren't really that much concerned about what people at home were thinking.

CL: *If you went in country were you adequately prepared and what was the most difficult adjustment you had to make?*

TG: Well, as I say, I was in the country twice there. I was completely prepared. And I, you have to, you have to remember now, it might have been different for somebody who was a draftee, a young soldier, someone who had just gotten thrown into it. I was someone who, that was my career, so I was completely prepared for it. I guess the hardest adjustment that we had to make was, at least the first time, was you know being in a totally different country, not being able to speak the language, not having any idea first hand what was going on with the people, and that took a great deal of an adjustment. But, as far as professionally goes, I was, militarily, I was completely prepared. Cause like I say, that's what I had been preparing to do for five years.

CL: *What did you understand the purpose of the American military presence in Southeast Asia to be?*

TG: Well, my, I guess basically my understanding was it was to prevent the communists from dictating to the South Vietnamese people what they would, how they would operate their country.

CL: *Were you engaged in combat and if so, describe that experience.*

TG: Well, I was engaged in combat on both the first time I was, as I say, I was the commander of a rifle company and then the second time I was an advisor to Marine, Vietnamese Marine battalions and brigades, so we were you know, engaged in combat on a day-to-day basis. So I, trying to describe what it's like's rather hard, it's, it's like most people have, it's been described before, certainly not original with me, it's, you go through days and days of, of nothing happening where you're just marching through the jungle and living in the swamps and nothing, then all of a sudden everything explodes and you have, you know, a minute, or an hour, or a day or two of just complete chaos and people being killed, and explosions, and everything going on. And then it all is over and you go back to, you know just sort of hours of just sort of largely nothing, but just sort of physically hardship conditions, but nothing, you know, no, no, nothing very exciting. . . .

Protests and Opinions on the War

CL: When did you become aware of the protests back home? Did you and your fellow soldiers talk about the war? about home? about your future plans?

TG: Well, we, you know, you became aware of it because obviously you could get the, you know, news broadcasts. They had an armed forces radio station, you could listen to the radio when you had a chance and that was broadcast on the radio news. Your family, friends sent you newspaper clippings, you know, magazines and that sort of thing. So you became aware of it, but that didn't have any first hand news. You know, my you know, again, I'm somewhat in a different position, my, my friends, the people that I would appear with were all professional marines. That was our career so we weren't, you know, we were busy fighting the war. I mean that was our job, that was our day-to-day thing so it was, that was what we talked about; fighting the war, more than, than anything else. I mean it wasn't as if, if we were, you know, we'd expected we'd eventually go back home, but we'd still be in the military, still be, as I ended up doing, training people to go to Vietnam. So . . .

CL: From here?

TG: Excuse me?

CL: *From back home, here or?*

TG: Yes. When I, when I came back from Vietnam I first went to school and then I went to Quantico [a military base in Virginia], where I was teaching Marine lieutenants at our basic school.

CL: *What was your personal view of the war and how, if so, did that change over time?*

TG: Well, my personal view, again what you have to realize, my personal view was that, you know, I was a professional soldier, I was in the military, you know my government had sent me over there to fight a war. So that was what I was doing, I was going over there to fight. I, my views changed quite a bit from my first to my second tour because my first tour, when I was over there I looked at the Vietnamese as probably not really caring very much about their country, not being willing to fight for their country. However, when I went, after I went to language school and could speak Vietnamese and went back there and served with them, that view changed completely and I found that my earlier views were completely wrong, I found the Vietnamese were both willing and capable of fighting for their country. So I, you know, I had no, I think we did a lot of stupid things over there in the war, but I don't think any of them, I don't think we were wrong to have been there, I think we went there with good intentions, I think we, what we were trying to do was the right thing. I think anybody that, that says that we were somehow morally wrong, hasn't read very much about communism, hasn't taken a look very much at what happened to that country after the communists won. So I don't have any problem with it, what we had done having been wrong, I think that we strategically and tactically made a lot of mistakes, which contributed to our defeat, but I, my views on that haven't changed.

A Parade at Last

David Donovan

After the end of the war, many of the men and women who had served during the Vietnam conflict remained bitter over what they perceived as public disinterest in the sacrifices they had made for the United States. The veterans of World War I and World War II had returned home heroes, but for Vietnam veterans there had been no such warm welcome. Many Americans were clearly ashamed by the Vietnam conflict. Supporters of the war lamented the United States' failure to prevent the North Vietnamese from conquering the south and seizing Saigon, while critics condemned U.S. support of a corrupt regime in South Vietnam.

Public attitudes toward Vietnam veterans did become more positive over time, however, especially after the building of the Vietnam Veterans Memorial in Washington, D.C., in the early 1980s. The memorial was designed by Maya Ying Lin, a native of Athens, Ohio, who was an undergraduate student at Yale University at the time. It consists of a highly polished black granite wall sunken into the earth and inscribed with the names of the fifty-eight thousand men and women who died in Vietnam. From one side the wall is almost invisible, as it lies beneath ground level; from the other side it is striking and powerful, with lists of names organized in chronological order by dates of death. While some were bothered by the dark nature of the wall— walking into the memorial feels almost like walking into an open grave—and some others were bothered by the age and ethnicity of the young Asian American designer, many visitors to the memorial found (and continue to find) the experience of visiting the wall reflective and healing.

The memorial was dedicated on November 13, 1982, at the end of an unprecedented week-long salute to Vietnam veterans that included speeches, rallies, and a parade. In this excerpt from *Once a Warrior King: Memoirs of an Officer in Vietnam*, "David Donovan" (the author used a pseudonym in writing the book) describes his feeling upon seeing the memorial and finally, at last, marching in a parade to welcome veterans home. Donovan served as a first lieutenant in the U.S. Army and was one of the officers sent to work as a military adviser in a remote district of Vietnam. As the commanding officer in that district, Donovan wielded enormous power and became, in his words, a "warrior king." Upon leaving the army Donovan returned to school and later became a professor of biological science.

In November 1982 I traveled to Washington, D.C., to take part in the Vietnam Veterans Memorial ceremonies. Thousands of other veterans were coming in from all across the country and I wanted to be there.

I wanted to go to the ceremonies for several reasons. I wanted to honor the dead, especially those I knew personally. I wanted to taste that old feeling of soldierly comradeship and sense of purpose that seemed so faint a memory. I wanted to see the memorial itself; I wanted to touch some of the names carved into its polished marble. And I wanted my damned parade.

On the first day of the activities I was one of many who participated at the National Cathedral in the reading of the names of all those who died in Vietnam. I was one of a long series of readers who would undertake a three-day candlelight vigil, continuously reading the names from the official casualty lists until all 57,937 had been read. I considered it an honor to participate in the ceremony and to speak the names of the dead into the quiet air of the vaulted cathedral.

We did our reading in pairs. My partner was an older man whose son had been killed in Vietnam. He and I read for half an hour and only went down the list from Bianconi to Blunkall. It was an emotional experience. Sometimes it was hard to continue reading because I would look out into the audience and see someone crying or wiping the tears from his eyes. A lump would swell in my throat and tears would blur my own vision. It brought home to me in a very stark way that I was speaking the names of real men who had had real families, real loves, and real aspirations. I was deeply moved by the atmosphere of the cathedral, the solemnity of the proceedings, and the deep expressions of sorrow. I was relieved that the time to honor our dead had finally come.

Gathering for the Opening of the Memorial

It was an intensely emotional experience to see all those GI's again. Thousands of them came into town in their old jungle fatigues or with some piece of an old uniform they had dragged out of the attic or closet. There were veterans there from every state in the Union. They came in by plane, train, auto, and bus. Some hitchhiked and some just plain hiked all the way from wherever. I didn't care what their service, what their unit, what their rank—I loved seeing every one of them. I think we all felt a strong sense of camaraderie. Every handshake included the symbolic thumb-grip of the brotherhood. Every man could feel like a hero.

Every veteran in town was looking for somebody he knew from the old days. Men would just mill around in the crowd, eyes darting from one face to the next. The emotions were guarded, and the eyes rarely showed any expression except the hope that the next face would draw that spark of recognition. When two old friends would finally find each other, the emotions would find release. There would be shouts, hugs, and tears as men who had shared their own corner of hell would meet again after more than a decade.

For those who couldn't find someone they actually knew, just finding someone from the same brigade or even the same division was enough. Men from the same unit, even if they didn't know each other personally, knew they had shared a common experience, a common terror, a common pain. It was not unusual to see two men standing braced in each others arms, sobbing out ten years' worth of anger, sorrow, and frustration.

Seeing the Vietnam Memorial

I went down to the Vietnam Veterans Memorial on the first day I was in town. That was the Wednesday before the official dedication on Saturday, November 13 [1982]. Veterans were just beginning to trickle into town for the weekend ahead, and we had just begun the reading of the list of the dead at the National Cathedral. I was prepared not to like the monument. I had seen drawings of it and had not been impressed, and I was aware of the sometimes harsh controversy surrounding its design. So I was pensive as I walked up the small rise on the Mall near the Lincoln Memorial. I knew that at the crest of the rise I would be able to look down into a slight depression and see the black marble walls of a large "V" pressed into the hillside. I knew that each polished slab that made up the chevron would have inscribed on it the densely packed names of all the men killed in Vietnam. I had already heard the place described with displeasure as "The Valley of Death." I wondered what my own reaction would be.

I reached the top of the rise and looked down. The black granite slashed starkly across the new grass. I stopped and just stood there for a few minutes, allowing myself to take it all in from a distance. I knew immediately that at least I didn't dislike it. It was solemn, it was indeed unadorned, and it carried no message other than the names of the dead. Yet it did not strike me as inappropriate. It was longer than I had imagined, and reminded me of a large artillery revetment. I wondered if others saw that same facet of the design.

I walked on down to the polished stones of the monument. A small crowd of other veterans was already there, standing quietly by themselves or talking in hushed tones in groups of two or three. Many were standing close to the wall itself, peering at the endless list of the dead and trying to find the name of a friend lost so long ago. Finding the names somehow brought relief. Gruff-looking men in old uniforms stared with red eyes and quivering chins as they found the names of those who had once stood by their side. Those who had been at the monument for a while and had gotten over the initial emotions went up and put their arms around those who had just arrived and were freshly hurting.

Seeing My Own Dead

I looked with dread for the names of my own dead. I was afraid that when my eyes fell upon them, they would leap off the black wall and strike me like a hammer. I was afraid of the pain. I was right. When I found their names I cried. It hurt so deeply to see those good names of long ago written so freshly on the wall of stone. I touched each name, trying to reach back to them across time and mortality. It was a way to shake their hands again, to hear their voices, to see their smiles, and to tell them that David Donovan remembered.

I must have stayed there for a couple of hours, just walking around, looking at faces, staring at the monument, going back to the special names I had found, letting it all soak in. The atmosphere was one of quiet, peace, and dignified respect for the dead. I sat alone for a long time on the grassy slope in front of the monument, thinking my own thoughts and analyzing my own emotions. I wanted to know if I should like this thing or dislike it.

Finally, I settled it. I walked away with a feeling of satisfaction; I liked it. There for all the world to see was a list of nearly fifty-eight thousand men who had died for a cause from which they could expect no benefit. The wall says one thing very clearly: If blood be the price of honor, then the veterans of Vietnam have surely paid enough.

Finally, a Parade

And I finally got my parade. For one day it was like being in the army again. It was Veterans Day, November 13. The word got around in crisp military terms: parade assembly time was 0845 hours. Old soldiers tried to remember how to fall in, dress right, and keep in step. Everyone was feeling so good that the fine points of parade technique didn't really matter. We were getting our parade! That was enough in itself.

The uniform of the day was old combat boots worn white with age, faded jungle fatigue shirts over old blue jeans, and service headgear of every description. On November 13, 1982, after more than ten years of waiting, the American Army of Vietnam moved out for its splendidly ragtag parade down Constitution Avenue.

As we made the sweeping left turn from the Mall onto Constitution Avenue, I could see clearly down the broad street. The sidewalks were crammed with cheering people. Since I was on the outside of the front rank, people reached out to shake my hand and pound my back. I wasn't special, I was just accessible. Men, women, and children were cheering and waving flags. The most common cheer was "Welcome home! Welcome home!" Our formation was more like a rambling cattle herd than soldiers on parade. It was so bad it was good and added to the joy of the occasion. Nobody was worried about anything, everybody was having a good time.

The swelling was in my chest again, the tears kept filling my eyes, but this time not from sadness—it was from pleasure and immense relief. A parade! For me. A great weight was lifted from my shoulders. Cheering crowds, smiling women, waving children—simple things really, but things soldiers have always yearned for and always will.

CHAPTER 4

Vietnam in Media
and Popular Culture

Reporting the War

Walter Cronkite

Vietnam was the first real "media war," and so helped usher in an era in which the public became used to seeing and identifying with trusted television reporters and news anchors. The most famous of all of these anchors was Walter Cronkite, who worked for many years as the *CBS Evening News* anchorman. Cronkite, whose trademark exit line was "and that's the way it is," was sometimes known as "Uncle Walter" and was once identified by a major poll as "the most trusted figure" in American public life. Millions of Americans remember that in 1963 it was a tearful Cronkite who informed the United States that President John Fitzgerald Kennedy had been shot, and millions similarly remember Cronkite shouting "Go, Baby, Go!" in 1969 as Apollo XI blasted off on the mission to land astronauts on the moon. Cronkite's name was so synonymous with trusted news reporting that for a while in Sweden news anchors were known as "Kronkiters" and in Holland as "Cronkiters." Americans learned their news from Cronkite, and took from him cues as to which issues and opinions mattered.

Cronkite was initially in favor of the war in Vietnam, although he did air reports critical of the war, including a famous video taken by CBS newsman Morley Safer of American soldiers burning down a South Vietnamese village with Zippo lighters. After returning from a short trip to Vietnam, however, Cronkite went on the air on February 27, 1968, and criticized the way in which the war was being fought. Abandoning his pre–Tet Offensive "hawkish" stance, Cronkite announced to his audience that it had become clear that "the bloody experience of Vietnam is a stalemate." To many observers at the time, it seemed that Cronkite's broadcast was a major contributing factor in Johnson's joint decisions to open up negotiations with the Vietnamese and not to run for reelection in 1968. In this excerpt from his 1997 autobiography *A Reporter's Life*, Cronkite describes how he gradually became disillusioned with the conflict and how he and his fellow journalists transmitted that sense of disillusionment to the American public through editorials and news reports. Cronkite retired from CBS in 1981, at which time President Jimmy Carter presented him with the Presidential Medal of Freedom, the highest award that can be given to a civilian.

We were in the early stages of this buildup [of U.S. forces] and were beginning to take our first casualties when I made my first trip to Vietnam. At this stage, Vietcong bombs were exploding with some frequency and with devastating results in the Saigon restaurants frequented by Americans. But the danger I had elected to face seemed to begin before I ever reached Saigon. As I boarded the Vietnamese airliner at Hong Kong, I was impressed by the efficiency of the boarding procedure and the cleanliness of the plane, but mostly by the beauty and charm of the stewardesses. Far from the hell of war, this was heaven.

Before takeoff one of the smiling, long-haired beauties handed me a copy of Saigon's English-language newspaper. A very black headline summarized the day's leading story: "Air Vietnam Stewardess Held in Airplane Bombing."

Was my stewardess's smile the smile of the cobra?

The flight was less relaxing than it had promised to be only a moment ago—and I learned the first, the fundamental, the elementary lesson about the Vietnam of the 1960s: One could not depend on things being what they seemed to be.

Saigon still retained some of the old French colonial charm that would soon disappear in the dust and smog of thousands of military vehicles crowding its once lovely tree-lined boulevards. The Caravelle Hotel, designated as press headquarters, was filling with correspondents and news bureaus, but many of us still stayed at the less modern and hence more gracious Continental Hotel across the square.

The roof garden of the Caravelle provided a box seat for the war. We watched the nightly bombing raids and gunship counterattacks on the city's outskirts, some nights more intense than others. One night, over to the northwest, five, six, maybe seven miles away, was a brilliant display of flares, lighting the countryside around. Tracers from unseen helicopters poured fire below, accompanied by the clump of mortars and the occasional bump and concussion of 500-pound bombs. The next morning Armed Forces Radio said that the U.S. command had reported there had been no important activity in Vietnam the night before.

The War Correspondents

A caste, or class, system that has always, I suppose, been applied to war correspondents to one degree or another has become more evident and more offensive with the growth of television. There are the grunts—the real battle reporters, cameramen and field producers who spend much of their time and risk their lives alongside the soldiers in the foxholes. Also there are the equivalents of the rear echelon troops—the bureau managers, broadcast producers, expediters—who man the base camp and seldom if ever see the real action. And then there are the anchorpeople, or, in the case of the writing press, the columnists, who spend a few days dipping their feet in the waters of war but who never suffer total immersion.

The members of this latter caste, influential as they are thought to be, are almost certainly going to be invited to dine with the generals and to have audiences with high officials in the host country. They are going to be offered escorted tours of the war—any war, whatever the war—and hence see a somewhat different war than those sharing the foxholes.

The danger is that they may believe this official version of events rather than what they are told by their own colleagues in the field. One can try to avoid falling into this trap, but it is not easy when duties on the home front necessarily limit one's visits to the war zones and thus one's exposure to the facts.

The damage can be limited by the VIP correspondent's own awareness of the problem, by his or her experience in previous or similar conflicts and by his or her determination to visit the foxholes and at least momentarily share the truth that is revealed with startling clarity out where the bullets fly.

Like most of us, I would rather have the approval of my colleagues than that of any other jury. That was particularly true with respect to our superb correspondents in Vietnam—and there were a legion of reporters, cameramen, soundmen and producers who risked their necks to get the story for CBS. I have some idea of what they thought of the visits of the 800-pound gorilla. As a young correspondent I held the same opinion of other gorillas in other wars. I would like to think that I conducted myself in Vietnam in such a way as to win at least some measure of approval from them.

I took advantage of the generals' dinners and the high-level political interviews, but I also made brief forays into what passed for the front lines in a war that had none. On that first visit I went out with the helicopter-borne 173rd Airborne Brigade, the first unit to be sent to Vietnam after the escalation from the military-observer stage. I rode with them into the jungle not far outside Saigon as they sought out the Vietcong to provide some sense of security for a city on whose outskirts, in those early days, the enemy appeared almost nightly. On subsequent visits I flew with the air support helicopters as they swept low over the jungle's treetops, machine-gunning whatever was under that green canopy, and I flew with the Air Force as it bombed that same jungle, where concentrations of the enemy were reported to be.

Feeling That We Were Making Progress

In the field and back in Saigon I heard the tales of the pacification officers who were working in the villages to win the hearts and minds of the people. While they acknowledged that they were not encountering much enthusiasm for democracy, as they had hoped, most of them had not yet sunk into the slough of cynical pessimism that would come later.

I was still impressed with our effort—impressed enough, as a matter of fact, to view with some embarrassment the performance of much of the press at the military's daily evening news briefing. While most of the older hands and experienced war correspondents appeared to be attempting in a rational way to extract the facts from the military and make sense of the daily communiqués, the younger reporters seemed to be engaged in a contest among themselves to determine who was the most cynical, who the most confrontational in their rude challenges to the appointed spokesmen. They struck me as attempting to defend the truth by branding every military statement as a lie.

I was not yet prepared to grasp the fact that Vietnam was no ordinary war as some of us senior correspondents had known it in World War II. This was no routine meeting of press and authority. I was not prepared for the ultimate truth: These hapless spokesmen were charged with explaining a war that had no explanation, and both they and the press knew this to be the awful truth. The press named the evening news briefing "the five o'-clock follies." It could have been the name for the war.

Despite all this, I returned from that first trip to Vietnam with the feeling that the evidence in the field seemed to support the contention of the high command and the administration in Washington that we were making progress.

The Evidence of Cam Ranh Bay

But then came the revelation of Cam Ranh Bay. That big open body of water was ringed by perhaps one of the most beautiful beaches in the world. The green forested hills wore the wide fine sands like a necklace. It was so perfect that many of us cynics suggested that it would be the postwar site of a chain of hotels—with casinos, of course.

That would have been a kind fate compared with that which fortune dealt the bay. The United States built a huge naval base there. Its roads and docks and warehouses, which covered almost 100 square miles, not only ruined the landscape; they provided the first physical evidence that perhaps the military didn't themselves believe the optimistic reports they were giving the administration and the country.

The building of that base was ordered in April 1965, when the administration had led congressional leaders to believe that our ultimate commitment of troops would be no more than 200,000. Yet the base was designed to service the other end of a pipeline that could handle many times that many troops. With Cam Ranh Bay my disillusionment began. That and the increasing reports from the military and the political foxholes of Vietnam that neither the battle to subjugate the Vietcong nor that to win over the Vietnamese villagers was meeting with any tangible success.

Additionally, there was something distinctly uncomfortable about a war in which it was impossible for even the most optimistic military spokesmen to claim that we were liberating and holding any sizable parts of the territory of South Vietnam. The criterion for success that our military adopted was the body count. The only way to measure victory, it seemed, was in terms of how many Vietcong we could kill. That was scarcely uplifting, scarcely inspiring, scarcely calculated to build the morale of either the fighting forces or the home front. It became increasingly difficult to justify the war as the terrible cost to ourselves in blood and material grew and the supply of Vietcong needing to be killed appeared inexhaustible.

Growing Disillusionment

At home my growing disillusionment was fed by the performance of President Johnson. He had long since made it his war. He adopted it officially when he invented or accepted that exaggerated version of the Gulf of Tonkin incident and with blustering indignation forced through Congress the Tonkin Gulf resolution. It gave him authority to conduct the war as he saw fit, and was, in effect, a formalization of the reality that the United States had taken over the conflict. For Johnson it was a personal challenge, almost a personal vendetta against the enemy. George [H.W.] Bush would later exhibit a similar trait in his military action against Noriega in Panama and Hussein in Iraq.

The extent of Johnson's personal involvement was brought home to me one night at the White House. There was some sort of late afternoon reception at which I was surprised to see Allan Shivers, a former Governor of Texas and not infrequent political adversary of the President's. The President came over to me at one point and said that Shivers was staying for dinner in the private quarters and he and Mrs. Johnson would like to have me stay as well.

There were just the four of us for dinner. The President was his most gracious to Shivers, and we had a pleasant time both before and after dinner sitting on the second-floor south porch that Truman had built despite a storm of architectural controversy. We talked—that is, *they* talked—mostly about Texas politics, which had fascinated me ever since I was a young cub reporter at the state capitol in Austin. Also, Shivers and Lady Bird Johnson had been just ahead of me at the state university there and we had much in common.

There was no doubt that Johnson was laying on his old enemy a pretty thick accounting of his duties, performance, prerogatives and powers as President. And then Vietnam came up.

As his hands drew in the air a picture of the action, I heard him say: "I'm going to bring my ships in here, and then, with my airplanes up here, I'm going to send my troops in." *His* ships, *his* planes, *his* troops. Maybe it was just a little braggadocio, one Texan to another, but what an astounding if unconscious revelation of his view of the conflict.

And Then Came Tet

My disillusionment was keeping pace with that of growing numbers of the American people. And then in 1968 came Tet.

The huge North Vietnamese–Vietcong offensive kicked off on the Asian New Year's Day, in violation of a holiday truce. Within days it had swept through every important city in South Vietnam except the big Marine base of Danang and Saigon itself. Even in Saigon the Communists were in the streets in some corners of town and had mounted a frightening suicide assault on the American Embassy in the heart of the city. According to reports, in scores of villages that we had considered pacified, the hearts and minds of the peasants had turned back to the Vietcong.

All of this even on the heels of more assertions from our military that the end of the Vietnam War was in sight, that they could clearly see the light at the end of the tunnel. Polls showed that the number of Americans who had sickened of the war and no longer had faith in the administration or the military that served it had become the majority. Demonstrations against the war spread from the campuses to middle-class communities across the nation as the Tet offensive brought public confidence to a new low.

I was proud of the degree to which we had kept our evening newscast free of bias, although on a subject as controversial as the war, we did not get credit from either side for doing so. The conservatives and government supporters thought we had joined the wild-eyed, "unpatriotic" liberals. The students and other war opponents branded us as mouthpieces for the establishment. I tried to keep our reports impartial but personally I tilted largely toward the dissidents because of the stridency of some of the conservatives in branding as unpatriotic those who opposed the war. Patriotism simply cannot be defined. Many of those against the war protested with the most dedicated patriotism—in the total conviction that the war was not a just one and was besmirching the image of a nation they loved.

"It Is Not the Journalist's Job to Be Patriotic"

In a misguided attempt to convince the administration leadership of the impartiality of CBS News, company president Arthur Taylor invited then Secretary of Defense James Schlesinger to a private luncheon with me in his office. The love feast collapsed before we had our first martini when Schlesinger invoked the need for patriotism on all fronts and I was unable to resist a probably too vociferous attack on the whole philosophy.

"It is not the journalist's job to be patriotic," I recall saying. "How can patriotism be determined anyway? Is patriotism simply agreeing unquestioningly with every action of one's government? Or might we define patriotism as having the courage to speak and act on those principles one thinks are best for the country, whether they are in accordance with the wishes of the government or not?

"It is everyone's duty to obey the laws of the land, but I think your definition of patriotism, Mr. Secretary, would preclude our listening to and reporting upon the opinions of those who believe your policies are inimical to the best interests of our nation. Perhaps these dissidents are the patriotic ones. At least they have the right to believe that their love of country is as sincere as yours, and that they have a right under our Constitution to speak their beliefs. And it is no breach of patriotism when we report on their behalf of a historic dialogue."

Taylor was moving toward the thirty-fifth-floor windows. He seemed to be contemplating jumping. Schlesinger was slack-jawed. He is a man of considerable learning who does not look kindly on those of lesser intelligence. It took him only a moment to recover his usual arrogance, and the lunch went on in the atmosphere he preferred—total dominance.

At the time of the Tet offensive, this was only part of the debate that was rending the American people. With the new uncertainties created by the Tet offensive, it seemed to me that perhaps we should put on the line that high level of trust which polls showed the people had in our broadcast. Perhaps, I proposed to our news president, Dick Salant, I should go to Vietnam as quickly as possible (the Tet offensive was still in full swing) and try to present an assessment of the situation as one who had not previously taken a public position on the war. Salant agreed, and that same night I was off for Asia.

Back to Vietnam

Back at the box seat to war on the roof of the Caravelle Hotel, I watched the helicopter gunships and bombers attacking suspected Vietcong concentrations on the city's outskirts and saw fires blossom on the docks downriver. I drove the several blocks from the city center to the Chinese section, which the Vietcong had penetrated, and I stood in the still-smoldering ruins they had left behind.

With producer Jeff Gralnick, cameraman Jimmy Wilson and soundman Bob Funk I flew and tracked with GI reinforcements into the ancient city of Hue, where the Marines were fighting house-to-house and where incoming artillery shook the command headquarters. It turned out to be harder to get out of Hue than to get in. Ambushes had closed the roads. We shared a helicopter out with the bags holding twelve Marines whose war had ended that day at Hue. I thought about them as, back in Saigon, I was assured by our leaders that now we had the enemy just where we wanted him, and with just a few more troops, 150,000 or 200,000, we could finish the job.

Tell that to the Marines, I thought—the Marines in the body bags on that helicopter. To me it sounded like more of the old siren song.

The official version: We had dealt the enemy a terrible blow, his offensive had failed and he was in retreat (although the cost to us and our South Vietnamese allies indeed had been extremely high in terms of men and materiel), and those once-pacified South Vietnam villages whose hearts and minds had proved so fickle were only being expedient in welcoming the Communists back—they would be back with us as soon as the areas were cleared.

As Tet wound down, I spent an evening up-country at the Phu Bai headquarters of General Creighton W. Abrams, Jr., the military's number two man in Vietnam, whom I had last seen in the World War II Battle of the Bulge as he fought to relieve the airborne troops in Bastogne. He was remarkably candid in admitting that the Tet attack had come as a surprise, and the serious extent of the damage, in casualties, materiel and morale. His officers joined us for a soft drink and their conversation brought home the nature of modern war as even the experience of battle itself had not. It was a highly and brutally technical discussion of fire power and kill ratios and the like. How, in effect, we could kill more Vietnamese. I wanted us to win the war, but this emotionless professionalism was hard to take.

But most incredible was the claim from on high at our Saigon headquarters that all we needed now was a few tens of thousands more men and we could finish the job. As it was, General William Westmoreland after Tet asked Johnson for another 206,000 troops. That would have meant 750,000 in Vietnam, three quarters of a million. Johnson said no, in effect closing the book on Lyndon Johnson's war. It would soon become Richard Nixon's war.

My decision was not difficult to reach. It had been taking shape, I realized, since Cam Ranh Bay. There was no way that this war could be justified any longer—a war whose purpose had never been adequately explained to the American people, to a people whose conscience burned because of the terribly, the fatally unequal sacrifice of the troops and the home front.

A Remarkable Broadcast

So I flew home and did a special report on the Tet offensive. It was as factual as we at CBS News could make it. But I ended it with a clearly labeled editorial. This was a radical departure from our normal practice. I had only once or twice stepped out of my role as an impartial newscaster, and on both those occasions I was defending freedom of the press on the theory that if we members of the press did not speak up for this democratic essential, no one else would.

As we discussed the broadcast, Salant warned that I was placing my reputation, as well as CBS's, on the line and that we were putting ourselves in jeopardy; that given the delicate state of the bitterly divided American public opinion, we might well lose a substantial part of our audience. I had no problem making my decision. Salant, as courageous as ever, agreed, although he was more aware than anyone else could have been of the troubles that might soon tumble around his head from disturbed, less courageous affiliated stations and thus perhaps his own management.

In the broadcast I made it clear that my subsequent words represented my own opinion and that this was an extraordinary affair. I said: "To say that we are closer to victory today is to believe, in the face of the evidence, the optimists who have been wrong in the past. To suggest we are on the edge of defeat is to yield to unreasonable pessimism. To say that we are mired in a stalemate seems the only realistic, yet unsatisfactory, conclusion. . . . It is increasingly clear to this reporter that the only rational way out, then, will be to negotiate, not as victors, but as an honorable people who lived up to their pledge to defend democracy, and did the best they could."

A Critical Reaction

The reaction to the broadcast was not at all what we expected. Although there were the usual letters of complaint from those who disagreed, they were not in unusual numbers. The newspaper editorials around the country reflected the previous views of their publishers.

There was no reaction from the administration, official or unofficial. I did not hear of, and I do not believe there were, any complaints from the White House to the CBS management, although in the past Lyndon Johnson had been quick to telephone me, and other anchorpeople, to complain of coverage to which he objected, and he was never shy about mentioning this to management.

The explanation came many months later, when we learned that the President was actually stunned by the broadcast. George Christian, the President's news secretary, and his assistant Bill Moyers, later to win fame on television, were present as the President and some of his staff watched the broadcast. "The President flipped off the set," Moyers recalled, "and said: 'If I've lost Cronkite, I've lost middle America.'"

I think it is possible that the President shared my opinion, and that, in effect, I had confirmed it for him. He probably had as much difficulty as I had in accepting the military's continued optimism in the face of the Tet setback.

The broadcast, I believe, was just one more straw in the increasing burden of Vietnam, and as such it added that much more weight to the decision which was forming in Lyndon Johnson's mind not to risk defeat in the forthcoming election. It was just five weeks after the broadcast that he announced that he would not be a candidate for reelection. David Halberstam would eventually write in his book *The Powers That Be* that it was the first time in history that an anchorman had declared a war over.

The Antiwar Theater

Joan Holden

One of the most striking and memorable aspects of American society during the Vietnam era was the existence of the counterculture. For Americans living at the time, the 1960s were in part defined by images of hippies, antiwar protesters, LSD guru Dr. Timothy Leary, and Abbie Hoffman and his "Yippies." The counterculture, as playwright and political activist Joan Holden noted, "was visible everywhere." As part of the counterculture, political theater and street-theater troupes began springing up in cities around the country; throughout the conflict street theater was an important and (in some parts of the country, at least) commonplace sight for many Americans.

Joan Holden was one of the most influential American playwrights of the second half of the twentieth century and was the principal playwright for the highly political San Francisco Mime Troupe (www.sfmt.org) from 1967 through 2000, when she retired in order to become a political organizer. In addition to over thirty plays she wrote for the troupe, she is the author of the 2002 theatrical adaptation of Barbara Ehrenreich's best-selling *Nickel and Dimed: On (Not) Getting By in America*. In this article, Holden describes what she observed of how the counterculture affected California in the middle of the 1960s and of how the political theater troupe with which she performed occasionally served as the catalyst for political protest. Like many of the most vocal antiwar activists, Holden explains, she was actually in favor of Ho Chi Minh and the North Vietnamese government, which she believed was participating in waging a "true national liberation struggle."

> Holden describes how she used her skills as a playwright and author to express her beliefs and to help organize campuses and neighborhoods against the war.

When I got back to Berkeley in 1966 it was like moving from black-and-white into Technicolor. It seemed to be a completely different world. Suddenly everybody was dressed like Indians. There was this whole new style that seemed to have burst out of nowhere—psychedelic posters and handbills, tie-dyed clothes, men with long hair, and people peddling underground newspapers. The counterculture was visible everywhere. It grew in the cracks, like dandelions pushing up through sidewalks. How could that have happened in two years?

It was amazing and wonderful, like arriving when the surf is high and just riding on it. There was so much to do—in art, music, theater, politics—it all merged together and it was all about asserting freedom in every medium and opening your mind to alternative possibilities. I never wanted to lead a "regular" life but till then I hadn't found a way out. At the same time, I've always been a puritan. I believe in doing socially useful work. The sixties showed me how to lead a life with purpose and joy; that you could do important work and have a great time doing it. All you had to do was wade in and be taken by this wave.

I never thought I'd hear myself say this, but drugs really played an important role, especially LSD. I never did much acid, but it didn't take much. It was an Alice in Wonderland experience—stepping through that little door—that gave you the sense you could cut loose from everything tying you down. Doing acid wasn't "self-medicating." It was about opening your mind, not dulling it. It was about tripping. That was a very important word.

Acting Up a Storm

When I got a chance to work for the San Francisco Mime Troupe it was a dream come true. It was come one, come all, join our carnival. But the carnival had a serious purpose. We wanted to create the best possible art about the most urgent issues, and blow people's minds by offering it to everyone, outdoors, for free.

In the forties and fifties we were raised to believe that there were no limits on what we could achieve in the future: a happy society, a fruitful land, technological paradise. In the sixties we translated those aspirations, but that feeling of immense and limitless possibility was the same. And the expanding economy made it possible to quit a job one week and get another the next when your money ran out. In 1967, I was living in North Beach in an apartment with a view of the bay for a hundred dollars a month. With roommates you could make it on twenty-five dollars a week. You didn't expect to make much money, but you could live really cheaply and do what needed to be done.

The right has successfully painted hippies as lazy. Actually, everybody worked like demons, just not nine to five. Theater is labor-intensive. At the Mime Troupe we worked ten to ten. We actually had to make a rule: "There shall be one day off a week."

A Play About War

We did three plays against the war between 1967 and 1971. Ronnie Davis, who founded the Troupe, was the director and he used to find old plays to adapt rather than waste time with inexperienced writers. My first show was an adaptation of an eighteenth-century Italian commedia dell'arte play by Goldoni, *L'Amant Militaire* [*The Soldier Lover*]. We used the French title—I don't know why. It's a typical plot about an old man wanting his daughter to marry for advantage and she wanting to marry for love. But it's set while the Spanish army is occupying Italy, two countries that could be taken for the U.S. and Vietnam. Into this play—this outrageous satire—we poured all of our energy and anger about the war. It was a very free adaptation. We pumped up all the values in the play and made the antiwar politics very clear. The captain became a general, the commander of the combined Spanish and Italian forces who was going to drive out the rebels with his next big offensive. He uses just the kind of twisted language we were hearing from

Westmoreland and Johnson about Vietnam. He says things like, "The fundamental policy of the Spanish government is to pursue peace with every available weapon" and "The rebels are on the defensive, as is proved by the growing number of their attacks."

Somehow, the idea developed that 1967 would be the "summer of love" and people should converge on San Francisco. And they did. But the Mime Troupe was not into "love." We were on the political end of the hippie-political continuum. We wanted to satirize the naïveté of the flower children. The hippie idea was you change the world by changing yourself and the radicals said you do it by changing institutions. So in *L'Amant* the general's daughter becomes a flower child who's convinced she can persuade him to change his ways and give up his arms. It doesn't work and she and her friends all get arrested and are about to be shot, till the servant girl dresses up as the pope and stops the war by decree.

The Theater as a Demonstration

We did these plays outdoors in parks or on college campuses, sometimes in front of thousands of people. As it happened, *L'Amant* toured the Big Ten midwestern campuses neck and neck with the Dow Chemical [job] recruiters. Dow made the napalm that was defoliating Vietnam and burning Vietnamese kids, so everywhere its recruiters went they were faced with big demonstrations and sit-ins. As word got out that this anti-war play was coming, we got huge, enthusiastic crowds. The play itself would become a demonstration. There was a character who would get the audience chanting, "Hell no, we won't go." In the parks, when we passed the hat after the performance we occasionally got a draft card.

We were also banned and picketed in a number of places. The debate over the war was ferocious. As much as we thought we were going to change history, we were always aware of serious opposition out there.

The Mime Troupe marched in every demonstration. We had our own marching band and wore these kind of ragtag mummer costumes. I played the triangle and cymbals. We had quite a range of songs—"When the Saints Come Marching In," "Louie Louie," "the *Marseillaise*," "The East Is Red," and "The Ballad of Ho Chi Minh."

[She sings]: "Ho Chi Minh was a deep sea sailor / Served his time out on the seven seas / Work and hardship were part of his early education / Exploitation his ABC's. Ho, Ho, Ho Chi Minh. . . ."

Those of us on the political side of freakdom knew that the Vietnamese were waging a true national liberation struggle and we really believed they "stole neither a needle nor a piece of thread from the people"—Mao's phrase. Our faith in Third World movements crashed against a lot of things in the course of the seventies and eighties. In my mind, though, the sixties didn't really end until Reagan was elected in 1980. There were bumps on the road, but it remained an enormously optimistic time until the end of the seventies.

Disgust at Protest Music

Joe McDonald

Music was one of the most important aspects of cultural life during the era of the Vietnam conflict, years that saw both the rise of rock and roll and the increasing importance of folk music as a form of mass protest. Certain songs, including Buffalo Springfield's 1966 "For What It's Worth," and Phil Ochs's 1964 "Draft Dodger Rag"—and on the other side of the issue Sergeant Barry Sadler's 1965 "Ballad of the Green Berets"—became enormously popular cultural icons and helped Americans to understand and express their feelings about living in the Vietnam era. One of the most influential songs of the period was the "I-Feel-Like-I'm-Fixin'-to-Die Rag," which was written by Joe McDonald and performed by his band, Country Joe and the Fish, at the great open-air concert at Woodstock in August 1969. McDonald, who wrote the song in about thirty minutes, has explained that in the song he attempts to place the blame for the war on politicians, businessmen, and even overly patriotic families rather than on the soldiers responsible for the fighting. The lyrics are sarcastic and the tone of the music is dark. (The song encourages "all of you big strong men" to come along because "Uncle Sam needs your help again." "So put down your books and pick up a gun," it continues, "We're gonna have a whole lot of fun.") The "I-Feel-Like I'm-Fixin'-to-Die Rag" spoke to many Americans and helped them to express their own frustrations with and fears of the conflict in Vietnam.

Country Joe's most famous—and most influential—performance of the "Fixin'-to-Die Rag" was that at Woodstock. In December 1969, several months after the festival, Country Joe and the Fish were asked to perform their famous song on the David Frost TV show, which was aired nationally during prime time. The letters included below were among the numerous letters sent to Frost by viewers who were disgusted and angered by the song and who condemned Frost for having such a "sick, unpatriotic" act on his show. Despite the feelings of those who wrote these letters, Country Joe's fame continued to mount. When the film of the Woodstock Festival was released in 1972, the "Fixin'-to-Die Rag" was featured prominently in the middle of the film, and the lyrics (highlighted by a "bouncing ball") were written across the bottom of the screen. The film —which proved to be immensely popular—thus brought McDonald's sardonic humor and profane message to the government and "establishment" to audiences around the world. Country Joe McDonald, who has released more than thirty-one albums, lives in Berkeley, California, maintains a Web site at www.countryjoe.com, and continues to perform around the country and the world.

December 20, 1969

Dear Mr. Frost:

It has taken me a week to compose myself after seeing your show with "Country Joe and the Fish." Did you stop to think that in your home audience there might have been mothers that lost sons in Viet Nam? "Be the first one on your block to have your boy come home in a box." We, here in the west know how bad the S.D.S. [Students for a Democratic Society] is. Is someone putting the pressure on you to expose left-wing extremists? You actually smiled and applauded those creatures when they finished.

The housewives doing their ironing in the late afternoon like to laugh and see pleasant things. You, Mr. Frost, are a bitter disappointment.

Mrs. W.A.
Concord, California

December 17, 1969

As a member of the silent majority, I was offended by the David Frost Show. It reached a new low in bad taste.

How any network could have permitted that "kettle of Fish" with their anti-American song and their unsightly garments to go before American public is incredible. It was the ultimate in ugliness to say the least. Mr. [Vice President Spiro] Agnew was right about the mass media. The whole show was a Frost.

L.L.D.
New York, NY

December 21, 1969

Dear Sir,

I would like to voice my objection to the singing group which appeared on the TV. They were a disgrace to this great country.

Mrs. R.J.
Springfield, Massachusetts

December 12, 1969

Mr. Frost,
The unbathed folk group who sang about Vietnam this morning should be shipped to any country of their choice. They are cowards of the worst degree. I'm proud to say my son fought and met the commies standing for freedom. He was shot 3 times. CBS should pay the folk singers to leave the country.

Mrs. S.D.
Provo, Utah

December 12, 1969

Dear Mr. Frost,

After seeing those things "the Fish" I felt like going to the bathroom and throwing up. Your show has hit rock bottom and you have just lost this viewer.

Mr. & Mrs. R.F.B.
Van Nuys, California

Sirs:

Shame—the dirty unkempt creeps (the Fish) and their song on Viet Nam were disgraceful. The weak audience applauded. We tuned you out for good. -TRASH - SCUM -

A former listener
The Commonwealth Motel
Boston, Massachusetts

December 6, 1969

Mr. Frost

I must protest vehemently your presentation of the obnoxious singing group called "Country Joe and the Fish" singing that repugnant song concerning the war in Viet Nam.

The lyrics appalled me especially the line: "be the first one on your block to have your boy come home in a box." In behalf of every mother whose son died in Viet Nam I am asking you in all humanity not to present these dirty unwashed people to us again with all their verbal diarrhea spewing from their filthy minds and mouths. I refuse to patronize any of the sponsors if this situation ever occurs again.

M.K.P.
Carbondale, Pennsylvania

December 5, 1969
Gentlemen,

Last night, December 4, 1969, the show was excellent except for the last few minutes. Why-oh-why did the beautiful interview with the Robbs have to be debased by a hoarse voiced, hairy unwashed creature giving forth with what I assumed was supposed to be a song?

I thought it was a most unfortunate finale to one of the otherwise best shows you have ever done.

Sincerely
E.L.A.
Bowie, Maryland

December 4, 1969

Dear David Frost,

We both have great respect for your show and watch it daily. We considered it great and high class. However today after [Lyndon Johnson's daughter] Lynda Bird and Charles Robb —how dare you give us that bearded slob who looks like a [Sharon] Tate [the movie star murdered by Charles Manson's followers] murderer!!!! he sang like an animal in pain!!!!!!! If you omit his kind, be assured your rating will not go down!

Sincerely
Mr. & Mrs. H.H
North Miami Beach, Florida

December 10, 1969

Dear Sirs:

I would like to register my disgust and horror at the number I'm watching at present on the David Frost Show, Wednesday, December 10th—the combo is called "Country Joe and the Fish" and the song "What Am I Fighting For?" at the dinner hour no less, when children are watching, it is blasphemous, disrespectful and anti-everything decent. I'm not for war but this is too much.

Mr. G.B.
Cleveland, Ohio

Mr. Frost,

I'm really disgusted with you for permitting that disgraceful song to be sung by those unkempt men or are they really women. I'm only 21 but these men embarrass me with their horrible appearance and shocking lyrics.

Yours truly
Mrs. F.C.
Bellerose, New York

1945

September 2: Ho Chi Minh, the leader of the Indochina Communist Party and the commander of the Communist guerrilla army known as the Vietminh, declares the independence of the Democratic Republic of Vietnam in Hanoi by quoting the American Declaration of Independence.

1950

The United States begins to subsidize the French in Vietnam while the Chinese Communists begin to supply weapons to the Vietminh (Communist guerrillas). By the end of the year, the United States is paying for half of the French war effort.

1952

November: Dwight David Eisenhower is elected president of the United States.

1954

April: In April, President Eisenhower formulates the domino theory in arguing that Indochina must be protected from Communist hegemony and Soviet and Chinese influence.

May 7: The French mountain fortress of Dien Bien Phu falls to the Vietminh forces commanded by General Vo Nguyen Giap. The defeat signals an end to French presence in Indochina. In July the Geneva Conference on Indochina divides Vietnam at the 17th parallel into North Vietnam under Communist rule and South Vietnam under Prime Minister Ngo Dinh Diem.

1955

January 12: Secretary of State John Foster Dulles first announces the doctrine of "massive retaliation," which threatens full-scale nuclear attack on the Soviet Union in response to Communist aggression anywhere in the world, including Vietnam. The United States continues to support Ngo Dinh Diem, who, in October, becomes president of the Republic of Vietnam (South Vietnam).

1959

July 8: America suffers its first combat deaths in Vietnam after an attack on the Bien Hoa barracks. By the end of 1959 there are nearly eight hundred American military advisers in Vietnam.

1960

November: John Fitzgerald Kennedy is elected president of the United States after promising to stand up to world communism.

December 20: North Vietnamese leaders form the National Liberation Front (NLF), which the South Vietnamese refer to as the Vietcong, in South Vietnam. By the end of the year approximately nine hundred American military advisers are in the country.

1961

June 4: After announcing in February that American advisers in Vietnam will return fire if fired upon, President Kennedy meets Soviet leader Nikita Khrushchev in Vienna and discusses American involvement in Vietnam. By the end of the year there are more than three thousand American military advisers in Vietnam.

1963

November 1: In a coup, Ngo Dinh Diem and his brother Ngo Dinh Nhu are removed from power by generals under Duong Van Minh and are executed. Although the United States does not initiate the coup, Ambassador Henry Cabot

Lodge knows of the revolution in advance and refuses to help Diem maintain power.

November 22: President Kennedy is assassinated in Dallas, and Lyndon Baines Johnson becomes president. By the end of the year there are 16,300 American advisers in South Vietnam and the South Vietnamese government is receiving $500 million in aid.

1964

August: On August 2 and 4 the U.S. destroyers *Maddox* and *Turner Joy* are allegedly attacked by North Vietnamese naval forces in the Gulf of Tonkin. In response, the Senate overwhelmingly passes the Gulf of Tonkin Resolution on August 7, authorizing the president to take any measures necessary to repel further attacks. President Johnson orders the bombing of North Vietnam. By the end of the year there are more than twenty-three thousand American advisers in South Vietnam.

1965

February–March: The United States begins Operation Rolling Thunder, the continual bombing of North Vietnam. In March the first American combat troops arrive in Vietnam.

April 17: The first major antiwar rally takes place in Washington, D.C., sponsored by the Students for a Democratic Society (SDS).

July 28: President Johnson approves General William Westmoreland's request for a massive increase in the number of U.S. troops in Vietnam. By the end of the year there are almost 185,000 U.S. troops in South Vietnam, and by the end of the following year there are 385,300 American troops in Vietnam.

1967

October–December: Protests against the war escalate. In October more than fifty thousand people march in Washington,

D.C. By the end of the year there are 485,600 American troops in South Vietnam.

1968

January 31: The Tet Offensive, a massive assault on American and South Vietnamese forces by the insurgents of the Vietcong, begins, shocking many Americans who had believed that the war was almost finished. The Vietcong take huge losses but reap enormous propaganda benefits.

March: On March 16 American forces massacre civilians at My Lai. On March 31 President Johnson announces that he is halting the bombing of North Vietnam and that he will not run for reelection.

November 5: Richard Milhous Nixon is elected president of the United States, defeating Vice President Hubert Humphrey, the Democrat nominee, and Senator Eugene McCarthy. Robert Kennedy, who had run for the Democratic nomination, was assassinated during the campaign. During the year American troop strength in Vietnam peaks at more than 536,000.

1969

March 18: President Nixon begins secret bombing of Cambodia as part of the war effort in Southeast Asia.

June 8: President Nixon announces the withdrawal of 25,000 troops from South Vietnam. By the end of the year there are 475,200 American troops in Vietnam.

1970

February 20: Secretary of State Henry Kissinger begins secret talks with North Vietnamese negotiator Le Duc Tho in Paris. By the end of the year there are 334,600 American troops in Vietnam.

May 4: Four students protesting against the war are killed by National Guardsmen at Kent State University in Ohio. The killings spark hundreds of protest activities at college campuses across the United States, and some of these protests are met with violence.

May 6: More than one hundred colleges are closed due to student riots over the invasion of Cambodia. By the end of 1971 there are under two hundred thousand American troops left in South Vietnam.

1972

February 21: President Nixon becomes the first U.S. president to visit China. The two countries issue a communiqué recognizing their "essential differences" while making it clear that "normalization of relations" is in all nations' best interests.

May 26: Nixon and Soviet leader Leonid Brezhnev sign the Strategic Arms Limitation Talks (SALT) treaty in Moscow, placing limits on certain types of nuclear missiles.

June 17: The Watergate scandal erupts in Washington, D.C., with the arrests of five suspected White House operatives.

November 7: Richard Nixon is reelected in a landslide, despite the Watergate scandal. The American withdrawal from Vietnam is almost complete. There are 24,200 American troops remaining in Vietnam.

1973

January 23: The United States, South Vietnam, and North Vietnam sign the Paris Peace Accords, ending the American combat role in the war. President Nixon announces that an agreement has been reached for "peace with honor." The U.S. military draft ends, and a cease-fire goes into effect five days later.

March 29: The last American combat troops leave Vietnam, and North Vietnam continues releasing all acknowledged American prisoners of war, some of whom have been held for eight years. By the end of the year American personnel in South Vietnam are restricted to those attached to the American embassy.

1974

August 9: Nixon resigns to avoid being impeached for attempting to cover up his complicity in the Watergate scandal. Gerald R. Ford replaces him as president.

September 16: Ford offers clemency to draft evaders and military deserters. Some irate veterans mail their combat medals to the president and burn their artificial limbs in protest.

1975

April 20–30: Amid scenes of massive chaos, Americans and South Vietnamese flee from the North Vietnamese. Saigon is captured by the North Vietnamese on April 30.

1979

August 15: *Apocalypse Now*, an emotional film about the Vietnam conflict, is released in theaters, inaugurating a series of popular films, books, and documentaries that seek to explore U.S. actions in Southeast Asia.

1982

November 13: The Vietnam Veterans Memorial is dedicated in Washington, D.C., at the end of a week of commemorations and parades.

Background/General History

Elizabeth Becker, *America's Vietnam War: A Narrative History*. New York: Clarion, 1992.

George C. Herring, *America's Longest War: The United States and Vietnam, 1950–1975*. 3rd ed. New York: McGraw-Hill, 1996.

Stanley Karnow, *Vietnam: A History*. New York: Penguin, 1984.

Neil Sheehan, *A Bright Shining Lie: John Paul Vann and America in Vietnam*. New York: Random House, 1988.

Soldiers and Journalists

Mark Baker, *Nam: The Vietnam War in the Words of the Men and Women Who Fought There*. New York: Morrow, 1981.

Philip Caputo, *A Rumor of War*. New York: Holt, Rinehart, and Winston, 1977.

David Donovan, *Once a Warrior King: Memoirs of an Officer in Vietnam*. New York: Ballantine Books, 1985.

Bernard Edelman, ed., *Dear America: Letters Home from Vietnam*. New York: Norton, 1985.

Stanley Goff and Robert Sanders, with Clark Smith, *Brothers: Black Soldiers in the Nam*. Novato, CA: Presidio, 1982.

Michael Herr, *Dispatches*. New York: Knopf, 1977.

Harold G. Moore and Joseph L. Galloway, *We Were Soldiers Once—and Young: Ia Drang, the Battle That Changed the War in Vietnam*. New York: Random House, 1992.

William Prochnau, *Once upon a Distant War*. New York: Times Books, 1995.

Tobias Wolff, *In Pharaoh's Army: Memories of the Lost War*. New York: Vintage Books, 1995.

Protesters, Objectors, and Activists

Dean Albertson, ed., *Rebels or Revolutionaries? Student Movements of the 1960's*. New York: Simon & Schuster, 1975.

Christopher Anderson, *Citizen Jane: The Turbulent Life of Jane Fonda*. New York: Holt, 1990.

Bill Ayers, *Fugitive Days: A Memoir*. Boston: Beacon, 2001.

Tom Hayden, *Reunion: A Memoir*. New York: Random House, 1988.

Alice Lynd, ed., *We Won't Go: Personal Accounts of War Objectors*. Boston: Beacon, 1968.

Benjamin Spock and Mitchell Zimmerman, *Dr. Spock on Vietnam*. New York: Dell, 1968.

Richard Stacewicz, *Winter Soldiers: An Oral History of the Vietnam Veterans Against the War*. New York: Twayne, 1997.

Howard Zinn, *You Can't Be Neutral on a Moving Train: A Personal History of Our Times*. Boston: Beacon, 1994.

U.S. Politics and Policy

Noam Chomsky, *Rethinking Camelot: JFK, the Vietnam War, and U.S. Political Culture*. Boston: South End, 1993.

David Halberstam, *The Best and the Brightest*. New York: Vintage Books, 1996.

———, *The Making of a Quagmire*. New York: Random House, 1964. Rev. ed. New York: Knopf, 1988.

Robert S. McNamara, with Brian Vandemark, *In Retrospect: The Tragedy and Lessons of Vietnam*. New York: Random House, 1995.

Norman Podhoretz, *Why We Were in Vietnam*. New York: Simon & Schuster, 1983.

Dean Rusk, as told to Richard Rusk, *As I Saw It*. New York: Penguin, 1991.

William J. Rust, *Kennedy in Vietnam*. New York: Scribner, 1985.

Arthur Schlesinger Jr., *A Thousand Days: John F. Kennedy in the White House*. Boston: Houghton Mifflin, 1965.

Vietnam and American Culture

Lee Andresen, *Battle Notes: Music of the Vietnam War*. Superior, WI: Savage Books, 2000.

Christian G. Appy, *Working-Class War: American Combat Soldiers and Vietnam*. Chapel Hill: University North Carolina Press, 1993.

Keith Beattie, *The Scar That Binds: American Culture and the Vietnam War*. New York: New York University Press, 1998.

Martin Binkin and Mark J. Eitelberg, *Blacks and the Military*. Washington, DC: Brookings Institution, 1982.

B.G. Burkett and Glenna Whitley, *Stolen Valor: How the Vietnam Generation Was Robbed of Its Heroes and Its History*. Dallas: Verity, 1998.

Arnold R. Issacs, *Vietnam Shadows: The War, Its Ghosts, and Its Legacy*. Baltimore: Johns Hopkins University Press, 1997.

Myra MacPherson, *Long Time Passing: Vietnam and the Haunted Generation*. Indianapolis: Indiana University Press, 2002.

Joan Morrison and Robert K. Morrison, eds., *From Camelot to Kent State: The Sixties Experience in the Words of Those Who Lived It*. New York: Oxford University Press, 2001.

Charles E. Neu, ed., *After Vietnam: Legacies of a Lost War*. Baltimore: Johns Hopkins University Press, 2000.

Online Resources

The *New York Times*'s 2000 Vietnam Retrospective (www.ny
times.com/library/world/asia/vietnam-war-index.html). This
Web site contains archived *New York Times* articles, online
interviews with journalists and pundits, and links to information on the Vietnam conflict, all gathered as part of the
New York Times's retrospective on the twenty-fifth anniver-
sary of the fall of Saigon.

The Oral History Project of the Vietnam Archive (www.viet
nam.ttu.edu/oralhistory). This project, which is based at
Texas Tech University, is dedicated to recording oral histories from participants, veterans, and observers of the conflict over U.S. involvement in Vietnam.

RE: Vietnam Stories Since the War (www.pbs.org/pov/stories/
vietnam/about.html). This site, which was developed by
P.O.V. Interactive, in cooperation with PBS Online, is de-
voted to gathering personal stories about the Vietnam conflict and especially about the years following the war.

The Veterans' Oral History Project (www.loc.gov/folklife/vets).
This project of the American Folklife Center at the Library
of Congress is dedicated to collecting and preserving oral
histories, along with documentary materials such as letters,
diaries, maps photographs, and home movies, of America's
war veterans and those who served in support of them. The
collection covers World War I and II, Korea, Vietnam, and
the Persian Gulf War.

Vietnam Veterans Memorial Online (www.nps.gov/vive/home.
htm). This is the government Web site of the Vietnam Veterans Memorial in Washington, D.C. The site contains information on the designing and building of the memorial and
on the scheduled events at the site.